# 1 MONTH OF FREE READING

## at

## www.ForgottenBooks.com

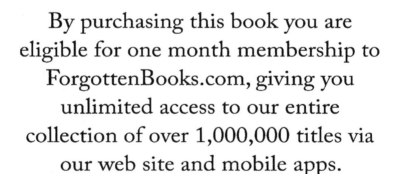

By purchasing this book you are eligible for one month membership to ForgottenBooks.com, giving you unlimited access to our entire collection of over 1,000,000 titles via our web site and mobile apps.

To claim your free month visit:

www.forgottenbooks.com/free1112450

ISBN 978-0-331-36640-2
PIBN 11112450

# Historic, Archive Document

Do not assume content reflects current scientific knowledge, policies, or practices.

# AMS report

**AGRICULTURAL MARKETING SERVICE**

**UNITED STATES DEPARTMENT OF AGRICULTURE**

AN ADMINISTRATIVE LETTER FOR AMS EMPLOYEES

JANUARY 1975

## Thoughts En Route

This morning as I walked to the bus stop, I noticed the trees. The new green of the past spring, the comforting canopy of leaves providing shade from the hot summer sun, and the riotous color of autumn are gone. Bare branches create a tracery against the sky, claiming to all who see a beauty of their own. Beneath them the trees are dormant, gathering strength for the seasons to come.

I wondered if we mortals also aren't affected by nature's processes. Sometime during each year, depending upon the customs of the people, there is a time for renewal, for looking forward, for assessing our hopes and aspirations for the year ahead. For each of us there is a new beginning. We shape it and mold it as best we can to our own liking. Somewhere in each form there is reflected our individual personalities marked by many facets of character: enthusiasm, ambition, integrity, attitudes toward our family, friends, and associates, acceptance of challenge, willingness to work, liking for our jobs, and all the nuances which make each of us a distinctive individual, a person unique.

It seems to me there is a somewhat similar process for AMS as a distinct and unique organization. We, too, have a shape, a character, a distinctiveness. All of us individuals who are in AMS together shape and express the character, colorations and attributes of this one agency in the constellation of government organizations.

The past year is history. This new year brings knowledge and, hopefully, wisdom from the past. It also brings challenges both known and unknown for the time ahead.

How will we respond? How do we wish to be regarded by those whose affairs we touch? What do we seek as the standard of our performance? These are not idle questions. The way we answer determines the degree to which we honor the public service of which we are a part, as well as the regard we have for ourselves.

I think our past points the way ahead. We seek by our performance to deserve the trust and confidence of the public we serve. We seek not to follow but to lead in setting a standard of excellence in the conduct of public programs. We seek the highest standards of professionalism; to be fully on top of our respective jobs, to find the best, most productive, least costly way to carry forward the programs for which we are responsible. We will welcome change, not for the sake of change, but to more effectively perform the tasks with which we are charged.

In going ahead with our work we will remember, too, that each person among us is important, is unique, and is due the human warmth and kindness by which each of us claim fellowship with those around us. And let us remember, too, as we now start another year, that alone no one of us can accomplish much, but that together we will accomplish a great deal; that together we will further honor the public service by continuing to earn for AMS the public trust and confidence that by our conduct it will deserve.

To each and every one a Happy and Satisfying New Year.

*E. W. Peterson*

**ADMINISTRATOR**

# AMS Profiles

## Jerry Foskett:

## Eastern Area Rep

## Dairy Market News

PHILADELPHIA—Jerry Foskett has never led a life of limited interests.

He's traveled extensively—46 of the 50 states—fought World War II in Africa and Italy, attended the theatre regularly, and maintained a number of hobbies and other cultural interests throughout the years.

Now all this in combination with a new job and its added responsibilities might seem a bit much. But that's what happened in August when Jerry was named eastern area representative for the Dairy Market News Service.

Foskett says he found the task before him challenging. That task: to paint an accurate picture of the marketing of dairy products on the eastern seaboard, an area that includes nearly half the consumers in the United States. The eastern seaboard draws its dairy products from all other regions of the country, as well as from foreign countries.

Now that he's been on the job some solid four months, Foskett says he likes it and hopes he's helping to provide information essential to the operation of an efficient marketing system. This system makes the buying and selling of milk and milk products an orderly process on which every-

one—dairy farmers, milk dealers, and consumers—can depend.

Foskett got his opportunity last July when AMS separated Dairy Market News from the Poultry Division, and set up a Dairy Market Information Branch within the Dairy Division.

Under the reorganization, a new Dairy Market News Office was established in Philadelphia, and Foskett, then dairy market reporter in Newark, N.J., was named eastern area representative.

Unlike his previous job in which he assembled facts and figures to form a dairy market picture of one state, New York, Foskett now found himself responsible for pulling together the details for a number of dairy products markets along the entire eastern seaboard. He was stimulated by the knowledge that he's helping lay the cornerstone of the program to be carried out by the new Branch.

Foskett talks daily with representatives of the industry—producers, wholesalers, distributors, retailers—and consumers. He collects and compiles facts on supply, demand, price, and the movement of milk, cream, butter, dry milk, cheese, and other dairy products.

This information is issued on Tuesdays, Thursdays and Fridays to subscribers, and to dairy market offices in Madison, Wis., San Francisco, Calif., and St. Paul, Minn., for republication and mailing to subscribers in the western and central areas of the country.

In addition, Foskett compiles and writes a national weekly and dry milk review that is mailed throughout the U.S. This is the only official USDA national report on that commodity.

The word "current" today often means "up-to-the-minute" rather than "daily." Up-to-the-minute, at least, is Foskett's meaning where dairy market news is concerned and for him, mail just doesn't always do the trick. So Foskett has been a strong advocate of a dial-a-phone operation (proven very successful in market news offices of all commodities across the country) to keep interested parties in touch with markets via telephone. He envisions dairy dial-the-news services eventually in Boston, New York City, Washington, D.C., Atlanta, and New Orleans.

Foskett is a graduate of the University of Vermont, and worked for the dairy industry four years as a quality control supervisor before joining the federal government in which he's worked for 24 years.  □

# Thackrey Retires: Saw 'Parade of History' in 39 Years

Ninety-four friends and relatives gathered with Information Division Director Franklin Thackrey and wife Jesse Tuesday night, Jan. 7, to help Mr. Thackrey close the books on 39 years of USDA service. The retirement dinner party was held in the Koran Room of Fort Myer's Patton Hall, in Arlington, Va.

Four of the five Thackrey children—Kent, 30, Maureen, 27, Sue, 24, and Keith, 21—flew and drove in from as far as San Diego to add their voices to those of their father's well-wishers. Daughter Janet, 36, who could not attend, sent her congratulations from California via a pre-recorded tape played during the evening.

The Dean of Information Directors, as Mr. Thackrey is known in USDA halls, joined USDA's Bureau of Agricultural Economics in 1935. In those years, he said, he considered Washington, D.C. a "madhouse," and even confided to a secretary that he "wouldn't go to Washington for love or money."

Mr. Thackrey recalls that just two months after he made that statement, in 1941, he accepted a job with the BAE's Division of Economic Information—in Washington.

In 1946 Orris Wells, chief of the BAE, named Mr. Thackrey head of the Information Division, a position which, despite years of renaming, program splits, reorganizations, additions, and subtractions, he maintained ever since.

In 1954 a part of the BAE combined with a part of the Production and Marketing Administration to form what became known as AMS Number 2. That yielded to the Consumer and Marketing Service in 1965, which became AMS Number 3 in 1972.

Mr. Thackrey bore witness to this parade of history, as he calls it, through eight Secretaries of Agriculture, from Henry Wallace through Earl Butz, and seven Presidents, from Franklin D. Roosevelt through Gerald Ford. His years of service took him through times of war—World War II, the Korean War, and the Vietnamese War—through dust bowls, depression, and inflation.

And what of changes in agriculture itself?

"There have been changes, of course, Mr. Thackrey said, "from extreme surpluses to worldwide demand for most everything that can be turned out." Mr. Thackrey notes the tremendous expansion in overseas markets and remembers the years when grain was stored in every possible place, including the World War II battleships, known as the "mothball fleet," on the Hudson River and in Norfolk.

Joining in the congratulations Tuesday evening were Mr. Thackrey's brother Russell; Wayne Dexter, retired director of the OMS Information Division and Mr. Thackrey's carpool chum of some 25 years; Bob McMillen, a speechwriter in the Office of the Director of Public Affairs; Director of the Office of Communication Claude Gifford; and Hal Lewis, retired director of the Office of Information.

Secretary Earl Butz sent his thoughts on the occasion in a letter read by Administrator Peterson: " . . . Thirty-nine years of devoted service is a long while. Our Congratulations and Thanks to to you for a job well done . . . It is the loyal and devoted efforts of great people like you that make the USDA the wonderful institution it is . . . '  □

# Division News

## Fruit and Vegetable

### ● Miller Speaks At Peanut Seminar

**Jim Miller,** assistant chief, Specialty Crops Branch, spoke on the Peanut Marketing Agreement at the National Peanut Council's Quality Assurance Seminar, in Chicago, Dec. 4. Other speakers included peanut butter manufacturers, Food and Drug Administration personnel, confectioners, and shellers.

### ● Extra Safety Measures At Terminal Markets

**Bill Crocker,** assistant officer-in-charge at the New York City Market News Office, says the New York City Police Department is providing more protection from criminal assaults and break-ins at the Hunts Point Market area. Foot patrolmen and two-man scooters now circuit the upper hallway level of the Hunts Point Market and the trading platform level below on a 24-hour basis.

In Louisville, Ky., floodlights have been installed on the terminal market to reduce the number of break-ins. According to **Les Matherly,** market news officer-in-charge, an 800-pound safe was recently wrestled across four sets of railroad tracks, including a main line, taken through a chain link fence and a swamp, but was later found unopened.

### ● Market News Dissemination Continues High

**Leonard Timm,** officer-in-charge at the Grand Forks, N.D., Market News Office, has convinced television stations Channel 11 and Channel 8 in Grand Forks to carry daily market news on their morning and evening broadcasts. Coverage began Nov. 7.

A telephone tape recorder was installed Nov. 4 in the Presque Isle, Me., Market News Office. All costs for the recorder, its operation and maintenance, are being paid by a local bank. Similarly, the tab for the recorder recently put into operation at the Riverhead, Long Island, N.Y., Market News Office, is being picked up by the John Deere Equipment Company outlet in Riverhead.

### ● John Boyle On The Air

**John Boyle,** in charge of the Presque Isle, Me., Market News Office, was a guest on the "Potato Pickers' Special," a radio-TV program presented by WAGM in Aroostock County during the potato harvest in November. WAGM provides a unique service to growers by broadcasting their harvest starting dates and specific needs for harvest labor and equipment throughout the area to field crews. Boyle and announcer Nate Churchhill, a former potato broker, discussed potato marketing during the show: John explained how the market news program works and the information available in the Presque Isle reports.

### ● Welch's Flower Coverage Complimented

George Beemer, manager of the Florida Flower Association in Fort Myers recently complimented **Jan Welch,** reporter, Orlando, Fla., Market News Office, on the quality and breadth of her coverage of the annual summary for 1973-74 on cut flowers and ferns. Jan handles all ornamental crops reporting in Florida.

### ● Dietitians Interested In Market News

**Bill Hines,** officer-in-charge, Cincinnati Market News Office, talked market news with a class of dietitians at the College of Mount St. Joseph in the Cincinnati area Nov. 21. The dietitians were interested in the role of market news, how reported prices are obtained, and tips on buying fresh fruits and vegetables.

On Nov. 20, 12 dietitian interns from New York Hospital toured the New York City's Hunts Point Market with **Tom Hill,** officer-in-charge. This tour has become a part of the regular training requirements, with special emphasis on identifying fresh fruits and vegetables.

### ● USDA Club Activities

**Jim Finazzo,** in charge of the New Orleans Market News Office, recently met with other USDA'ers in the area, including Thomas Kuhn, director of the New

# Division News

Orleans Computer Center, and Dr. John Barber, director of the Southern Forest Experiment Station, in the interest of forming a New Orleans USDA club.

## ● Visitors

**New York City Market News Office** - Hsióh-Chung Lu, senior specialist, Agricultural Technical Mission of the Republic of China, Taiwan, and 20 Economics graduate students from the New York University visited the office and toured the Hunts Point Market Nov. 4. **Tom Hill**, officer-in-charge, explained the function and role of market news in the marketing system. On Nov. 13 Harold F. Young, chief designer, Ashton Containers Limited of Bristol, England, visited the office. Young was interested in containers for commodities being shipped from the Caribbean area, as well as those used in the United States.

**New Orleans, La., Market News Office** - After her tour of market facilities with **Jim Finazzo**, officer-in-charge, Margaret Barron, home economics agent, Louisiana Cooperative Extension Service, prepared an article for the *New Orleans Times Picayune*. The article described the availability of fresh fruits and vegetables from all parts of the world and market news' role providing information on the arrivals and wholesale prices of fresh produce.

## ● Recent Grading Demonstrations

**C. A. Roundy,** area officer-in-charge, PPSI Branch, Los Angeles, and **Frank Warren,** sub-area supervisor, conducted the annual three-day grading demonstration Oct. 1-3, for the Food Buyers Class, Food and Nutrition Department of the California State Polytechnic University, Pomona, Calif. Twenty-three students attended the sessions each day. Roundy and Warren explained the Branch's inspection services.

**Dick Mier,** inspector, PPSI Branch, met with the University of Wisconsin, River Falls Food Science Class Oct. 21, to discuss the Branch services and demonstrate the grading procedures of several canned vegetables. The university students and instructors showed keen interest in the demonstration and actively participated in the product grading.

**Tom Crider,** standardization specialist, PPSI Branch, demonstrated product grading using both variable and attribute standards at the Advanced Food Management Class, U.S. Army Quartermaster School, Fort Lee, Va., Nov. 13. Crider also described the services provided by the Branch, and the development and use of U.S. grade standards.

◀

*Residents of the San Juan*
*office housing the headquarters of the*
*Texas-Federal Inspection Service and the Texas*
*Department of Agriculture were particularly*
*proud of their Christmas window this year, and sent*
*this picture in to show why. Under cooperative*
*agreement the Service is supervised by the Fresh*
*Products Standardization and Inspection Branch.*

# Division News

On Nov. 15, **Joe Scarbrough,** resident processed fruit and vegetable inspector, Kansas City, Kan., met with 26 students from the K-State Foodservice Systems Class. Scarbrough demonstrated the grading of frozen french fried potatoes and explained the Branch's inspection and standardization activities. Students in the Foodservice Systems Class each year visit cafeterias, restaurants, warehousing facilities and the USDA Processed Products Standardization and Inspection Branch laboratory in Kansas City.

● **Recent Meetings—Standardization and Inspection Branches**

**Pat Lively,** Baltimore area officer-in-charge, PPSI Branch, spoke before 50 Food and Drug Administration investigators at their District Conference in Baltimore Oct. 29. Ms. Lively discussed the inspection, standardization and technical services of the Branch and the availability of these services to the food processing industry. She devoted much of her presentation to reviewing the specific responsibilities of USDA inspectors and FDA investigators covered in the AMS-FDA Memorandum of Agreement.

**Mark Grant,** East Point, Ga., area officer-in-charge, PPSI Branch, met with the Clemson University Residue Committee at Charleston, S.C., Oct. 31, to present the Branch's aflatoxin program. The Clemson committee is composed of representatives of State, city, and federal agencies who meet quarterly to discuss areas of mutual concern in the peanut industry.

**Harley Watts,** Van Wert, Ohio, officer-in-charge, PPSI Branch, attended the Indiana Canners Association meeting Nov. 6, in Fort Wayne, Ind. Watts reports the review session on new processing tomato varieties grown at Purdue University, and the session covering food surveillance by FDA inspectors were particularly interesting.

**Jack Barham,** area officer-in-charge, Ripon, Wis., PPSI Branch, attended the Wisconsin Canners and Freezers Association Convention in Milwaukee Nov. 19-20. Barham met individually with management from several Wisconsin and Minnesota companies who were interested in the new Quality Assurance Program Services now offered by the Branch.

**Paul Beattie,** Fresh Products Standardization and Inspection Branch (FPSI), Standardization Section, has met with market receivers in New York City to discuss the proposed combining of the onion standards.

Standardization staff members have met with representatives of the John Henry Company, Lansing, Mich., and the United Fresh Fruit and Vegetable Association to discuss the development of the tomato color chart visual aid and the proposed licensing of John Henry to sell USDA visual aids to the public.

**Donald Matheson,** chief, FPSI Branch, was in Florida Nov. 9-15 attending the Peanut Butter Manufacturers and Nut Salters Association Convention in Pappas. While in Florida Matheson also conferred with federal-state supervisors and reviewed inspection operations.

**M.C. Erickson,** western regional supervisor, FPSI Branch, was in Hawaii Nov. 13-22 attending the Western Growers Association Convention and reviewing inspection operations.

## Livestock

● **Cecil R. Cowart,** supervisory meat grader at Memphis, Tenn., died on Nov. 15. He joined the Meat Grading Branch at Thomasville, Ga., in 1957, and subsequently worked at Tuscaloosa, Ala.; Montgomery, Ala.; Jacksonville, Fla.; Kansas City, Mo.; and Bell, Calif. Cowart was transferred to Memphis in 1972.

● **November '74 Training Class**

The six trainess in the November 1974 training class reported to their first field stations for on-the-job training, Nov. 18. They completed a two-week orientation program at Columbus, Ohio, Nov. 4-15. Following usual procedure, the orientation sessions were held on

# Division News

the Ohio State University campus and the trainees also used meatpacking facilities in the Columbus area.

The trainees, their colleges, and field locations are: **Dennis L. Garton** (Michigan State University), Chicago, Ill.; **Ann Marie Hritzak** (Michigan State U.), Omaha, Neb.; **Mark R. Longo** (U. of Connecticut), Omaha, Neb.; **Billy G. McCalla** (Prairie View A&M), Denver, Colo.; **Rudy Ramirez** (U. of Arizona), Sioux City, Iowa; and **Paul A. Swint** (West Texas State U.), Dallas, Tex.

## ● BCDS Goes Automated

To increase efficiency, the processing of Beef Carcass Data Service (BCDS) forms was automated Nov. 1. Details of the computer processing system were developed by the Meat Grading Branch and Technical Services Division. The new automated program is under the direction of **Gary Benton,** Meat Grading Branch management technician. The program saves an estimated 75 percent of the time previously required for manual handling.

Approximately 95,000 official BCDS eartags have been distributed to 33 cooperating cattlemen's and agricultural groups since the BCDS went nationwide in August 1972. The cooperating groups in turn distribute the eartags to producers and feeders. Meat graders evaluate the carcasses of BCDS-eartagged cattle and record the quality grade and other value-determining characteristics. The data then goes to the tag purchaser. To date, carcass data has been collected on 15,300 cattle.

## ● Market News Office Relocates

The Market News Branch Office in Nashville, Tenn., moved Dec. 1 from the Nashville Union Stockyards Building to the State Department of Agriculture headquarters in the same city. The Stockyards were closed Nov. 30, a victim of rising overhead costs and declining market receipts. **Samuel Wooten,** reporter in charge of the Nashville office, will now have more time to personally supervise the extensive Federal-State market news program in Tennessee, which includes graded feeder pig sales, special feeder cattle sales, and livestock auctions throughout the state.

## ● Briefings On Beef Grading Proposal Held in Six Cities

More than 400 consumer and industry representatives, and members of the press attended six regional briefings—in Washington, New York City, Chicago, Dallas, Atlanta, and San Francisco—held between Oct. 8 and Nov. 11 to explain how the public would be affected if the Division's proposed changes in beef grades are adopted. Officials discussing the proposed changes at the briefings included Administrator **Ervin Peterson**, Assistant to the Secretary for Consumer Affairs **Nancy Steorts**, Livestock Division Director **John Pierce**, and Standardization Branch Chief **Ned Tyler**. **Jerry Mason**, formerly of the Information Division, handled all advance work for the briefings.

The beef grading proposal was originally announced on Sept. 10, and the deadline for comments from the public was Dec. 10. Livestock Division personnel are carefully evaluating all comments received.

## ● Sheep Producers Say "Yes" On Referendum

For the sixth time since 1954, U.S. sheep producers and feeders have voted to continue supporting promotional activities to increase consumer awareness of lamb and wool. Held Nov. 4-15, the nationwide referendum was called by the Secretary of Agriculture, who is authorized to call for such a vote each time the National Wool Act of 1954 is extended. The promotional program is conducted by the American Sheep Producers Council and is monitored by the Livestock Division. Promotional funds will be deducted from USDA price support payments which producers may receive on 1974-77 wool marketings.

Results of the referendum were announced Nov. 27 by ASCS, which conducted the balloting.

## ● Earl Johnson Addresses Exposition

Meat Grading Branch Assistant Chief **Earl Johnson** was guest speaker at the 59th International Hotel and Motel Educational Exposition in New York City,

# Division News

Nov. 13. He discussed current and proposed beef grade standards and the USDA meat acceptance service, and presented the USDA slide series *How To Buy Beef*.

## ● Fulton Grades Carcasses At State Fair

**Bill Fulton,** market reporter in charge of the Federal-State Market News Office in Little Rock, Ark., graded beef and hog carcasses for the Future Farmers of America (FFA) carcass contest at the Arkansas State Fair, Oct. 8-9. He was assisted by **Terry Warner,** meat grader stationed at Memphis, Tenn., and two Extension Service employees. Some 113 hogs and 92 cattle were entered in the contest.

## Poultry

## ● Grading Branch Supervisors Meet

Administrative and technical matters were discussed at a November meeting of Federal-State supervisors and their assistants from the San Francisco and Des Moines regions. Grading Branch Regional Directors, their assistants, and members of the Division's National (Washington) Office also attended the session, held in Dallas, Tex., Nov. 18-22.

The Chicago and Philadelphia regions will hold a joint meeting in Memphis, Tenn., Jan. 13-17.

## ● Order Being Drafted on H. R. 12000

Division personnel have been working with an industry committee assigned the drafting of a proposed order on the Egg Research and Consumer Information Act. The proposed order, along with a request to hold a hearing, is to be presented to the Secretary of Agriculture.

Following public hearing and approval by egg producers, the Secretary would implement the provisions of the Act, which was signed by President Ford Oct. 1. The law would enable egg producers to carry out a coordinated program of research and education to improve their markets for eggs, egg products, and spent fowl (fowl no longer laying), by assessing themselves up to 5 cents per case of shell eggs marketed.

## ● Skinner Holds Training Sessions for Graders

National Poultry Supervisor **Jim Skinner** has already held four in a series of two-day off-the-job training sessions for all poultry graders. The sessions, which Skinner began in November, will be held throughout the country through June.

## ● *Broiler Marketing Facts* **Issued**

*Broiler Marketing Facts* covering the second quarter of 1975 was released in the early part of December. The publication was prepared by the Poultry Division with assistance from economists and marketing specialists in other USDA agencies. *Broiler Marketing Facts* helps the broiler industry plan production and marketing so an adequate supply of broilers is marketed at reasonable prices to producers and consumers.

## ● Nichols Attends ARS Poultry Workshop

Standardization Assistant Branch Chief **Merlin Nichols** attended the ARS-sponsored workshop, "Study of Programs Involving Poultry Product Quality As Affected by Management, Stress, Nutrition and Health," during the week of Oct. 28 near the Research Center in Beltsville. Discussions centered around necessary basic research.

## ● Handy Attends FDLI - FDA Educational Conference

Home Economist **Betty Handy** attended the Eighteenth Annual Educational Conference sponsored by the Food and Drug Law Institute in cooperation with the Food and Drug Administration in Washington, D.C., during the week of Dec. 2. Discussions focused on current congressional and legal/regulatory developments affecting food, including safety assurance, inspection, penalties, registration and labeling.

# Division News

## Transportation and Warehouse

### ● Getting Three Birds with One Stone

The Warehouse Service Branch is getting three birds with one stone.

**Dick Thune** and **Glenn Shelgren,** the Minneapolis Area's two Montana-based examiners, are on a two-week loan to work with Portland Area Office exam-iners. The Portland Area temporarily needs some help in Idaho to examine a multi-elevator complex. Dick and Glenn are nearer to the work than are the Portland examiners, and they'll benefit from the experience of examining federally licensed elevators.

As a result **J. Gordon Shields,** officer-in-charge, Portland, will achieve his examination goal and, as a side benefit, will save on travel costs. The cake is iced with an exchange of ideas among the examiners of the two areas involved.

*Indianapolis area warehouse examiners pause during annual conference and pose for photo for the record. (Story next page.)*

9

# Division News

## ● Iowa-AMS Cooperative Agreement

Director **Jim Lauth** and Warehouse Service Branch Chief **Jerry Oien** met with the Iowa Commerce Commission in Des Moines, Nov. 19, to discuss operations under a cooperative warehouse examination agreement between Iowa and AMS. Under the agreement, Iowa provides a specified number of state examiners who work with federal examiners under AMS supervision. The examinations performed by the combined staff serve both state and federal purposes. Meeting partcipants found just one change necessary: Iowa will furnish one additional examiner to accomplish its part of the workload.

## ● Indianapolis Warehouse Examiners Meet

Warehouse examiners of the Indianapolis area of the Warehouse Service Branch met at an annual conference conducted by Officer-in-Charge **Harry Wishmire** in Indianapolis on Nov. 5-7. The meeting, a balance of "in-house" talent and outside speakers, highlighted for the examiners the many changes taking place in the grain warehousing industry.

A keynote speaker was Ralph B. Hampton, vice president and treasurer of the St. Louis Bank for Cooperatives, St. Louis, Mo. Hampton covered the financing of grains and the reliance of financial institutions upon audits performed by the examiners. He emphasized that changing marketing patterns are placing more demand on the elevators for sound financing. For example, he said, instead of USDA, now farmers, merchants, and local elevator operators are carrying inventories. Hampton said his bank lends $100 million monthly with about $482 million currently outstanding. The St. Louis Bank for Cooperatives maintains a staff of only 25 people and therefore must largely rely upon the audits performed by the AMS examiners to insure that the loans are sound.

## ● Wishmire at "Warehouse Receipts Financing" Conference

**Wishmire** also participated in a mid-November workshop, "Warehouse Receipts Financing," held in connection with the 23rd National Agricultural and Rural Affairs Conference, Agricultural Banker Division, American Bankers Association. Wishmire recapped the auditing procedures for warehouses licensed under the U.S. Warehouse Act. Bankers in the country's major production areas rely heavily upon examinations made by AMS examiners as a source of protection for investments in commodity markets.

# Personnel Actions

## RETIREMENTS

### Livestock

**Max Fairman,** meat grader stationed at West Fargo, N.D., retired on disability Nov. 6. Fairman joined the Meat Grading Branch in 1961 at Denver, Colo., and he also worked at Spencer, Iowa, and South St. Paul, Minn., before his transfer to West Fargo in 1973.

**Arthur W. Stevens,** a livestock and meat marketing specialist in the Standardization Branch, retired Nov. 30. Stevens joined the Livestock Division in 1967 after 34 years of industry experience in meat processing.

# Personnel Actions

## Information

Franklin Thackrey, who has been with USDA for 39 years, and director of the Information Division for 28 years, retired Dec. 31.

## WELCOME

### Cotton

Joan E. Meserve, clerk-typist, Administrative Group, Washington, D.C.

Janet A Ring, chief clerk, Cotton Classing Office, Little Rock, Ark.

### Fruit and Vegetable

Evelyn LaPorte reported for work as clerk-typist in the New York Market News Office Nov. 20.

Libby Pannell, clerk-typist, joined the Complaint Section of the Regulatory Branch Nov. 25.

Melvin Stanard, clerk-typist, entered on duty in the Dockets and Records Control Unit of the Regulatory Branch Dec. 2.

### Grain

Robert Chapman, physical science aide, joined the Commodity Inspection Branch in Beltsville Oct. 27.

David Fulk, food technologist, joined the Standardization Branch, Hyattsville, Sept. 29.

Donald Jump, budget & accounting specialist, joined the Administrative Office, Hyattsville, Sept. 29.

Clarice White, clerk-typist, joined the Fort Worth field office Oct. 27.

### Livestock

Ronald E. Matheson, meat grader, was reinstated at Bell, Calif., on Nov. 25.

### Poultry

Marie Bush, agricultural commodity grader (ACG), Grading Branch, Fairhope, Ala., Nov. 10.

Clarence Gerling, supervisory agricultural commodity grader, Grading Branch, Columbus, Ohio, Nov. 1.

Lorraine E. Harper, clerk-typist, Market News, Newark, N.J., Oct. 27.

Susan Howard, secretary-steno, Standardization Branch, Washington, D.C., Nov. 10.

Henrietta D. Lubetski, secretary-steno, Marketing Programs Branch, Washington, D.C., Nov. 24.

Edward A. Plante, (ACG), Grading Branch, Boston, Mass., Nov. 24.

## RESIGNED

### Grain

Goldia White, clerk-typist, Mobile, Ala., field office.

### Poultry

Mary F. Begley, secretary-steno, Marketing Programs Branch, Washington, D.C., Nov. 8.

Thaddeus Price, (ACG), Arlington, Tex:, Nov. 30.

John E. Sulouff, (ACG), Freehold, N.J., joined the Division in 1968.

Jewel C. Watkins, (ACG), Roanoke, Ind., Nov. 23.

## TRANSITION

### Fruit and Vegetable

Michael A. Canon, inspector, Fresh Products Standardization and Inspection Branch, Chicago Terminal Market, was reassigned to the Standardization Section, Washington, D.C., Dec. 8.

Betty Gaither, who had transferred to Fresh Products Standardization and Inspection, returned to her previous assignment as secretary to the Market News branch chief on Nov. 25.

Mike Golightly, inspector, Fresh Products Standardization and Inspection Branch, from Milan, Ill., to Chicago,. Ill., Nov. 1.

George Hamilton, inspector, Fresh Products Standardization and Inspection Branch, from Chicago, Ill., to Milan, Ill., Nov. 1.

Rebecca Kizer, formerly clerk-typist for the Washington, D.C., market reporter, returned to Market News Dec. 9 to become a clerk-typist in the Market Reports Section after a short period with the Information Division.

Mary O. McIntyre, secretary-steno, Washington, D.C., transferred Nov. 10 to the National Park Service in Denver, Colo.

Wilbur Whatley, inspector, Fresh Products Standardization and Inspection Branch, reassigned from night supervisor to assistant officer-in-charge, New York Terminal Market, Dec. 8.

### Grain

Robert Albert, chief of the Standardization Branch, has transferred to the position of assistant to the director (training & recruiting officer).

# Personnel Actions

Marty Lewis, clerk-steno, transferred from the Commodity Inspection Branch, Hyattsville, to the Program Analysis Group, Hyattsville, Oct. 27

Ron Roberson, grain marketing specialist, transferred from the Standardization Branch, Hyattsville, to the Poultry Division Oct. 13.

### Livestock

Robert Eastes - Roswell, N.M., to Albuquerque, N.M.
Donald D. Powers - Omaha, Neb., to Amarillo, Tex.
Eddy W. Tittle - Sioux City, Iowa, to Lubbock, Tex.
Jerry T. Willard - Omaha, Neb., to Amarillo, Tex.

### Poultry

The following agricultural commodity graders have transferred within the Grading Branch:

Mary Jewell Anderson - Cullman to Empire, Ala., Nov. 10.
Raymond P. Bair - Seymour to Wabash, Ind., Nov. 3.
Florence Gould - Griswold to Elk Horn, Iowa, Nov. 24.
Jerry C. Horton - Canton to Terry, Miss., Nov. 10.
Samuel R. Lambert - Huntsville to Berryville, Ark., Nov. 5.
Annette G. Parker - Morton to Canton, Miss., Nov. 10.
Bessie Sweeting - Birmingham to Ashland, Ala., Nov. 3.

### Technical Services

Jo Witteveen has transferred from the Office of the Secretary to the Management Services Group where she will be a management analyst trainee.

## PROMOTIONS

### Fruit and Vegetable

Samual Boltax, Fresh Products Standardization and Inspection Branch, promoted to night supervisor, New York City Terminal Market, Dec. 8.

Carmine J. Cavello, Fresh Products Standardization and Inspection Branch, was promoted from assistant to officer-in-charge, New York City Terminal Market, Dec. 8.

Frank J. McNeal, Fresh Products Standardization and Inspection Branch, officer-in-charge, New York City Terminal Market, was reassigned and promoted to assistant head of the Standardization Section, Washington, D.C., Nov. 24.

### Poultry

Keith G. Salmi, agricultural commodity grader, Grading Branch, Harrisburg, Pa., was promoted to supervisory agricultural commodity grader, Harrisburg, Pa., Nov. 10.

## AWARDS

### Grain

### Length of Service Awards

35 years

Vera L. Colbry, Sacramento, Calif.
W. Haward Hunt, Hyattsville, Md.
C. Adele Johnson, Spokane, Wash.

30 years

Arthur W. Barstad, St. Louis, Mo.
Richard W. Gallup, Hyattsville, Md.
Harold W. Heins, Minneapolis, Minn.
Alex E. Hueseman, St. Louis, Mo.
George T. Lipscomb, Hyattsville, Md.
Carl J. Matel, Duluth, Minn.
Earline D. 'Murrell, Crowley, La.
Harold F. Newstead, Jr., Baltimore, Md.
John L. O'Brate, Hyattsville, Md.
Lee G. J. Regan, Stuttgart, Ark.
Harry H. Schmidt, New Orleans, La.
Edgar W. Sundermeyer, Beltsville, Md.
William T. Wisbeck, Hyattsville, Md.

25 years

Milton E. Blust, New Orleans, La.
James H. Byrd, Montgomery, Ala.
H. Hackett Cook, New Orleans, La.
Clyde R. Edwards, Hyattsville, Md.
Charles C. Groves, Jonesboro, Ark.
Robert W. Probst, Mobile, Ala.
Robert L. Roberts, Houston, Tex.
Marion L. Stroh, Indianapolis, Ind.
Samuel P. Washington, Hyattsville, Md.
Bobby G. Wright, Portland, Ore.

20 years

Maurive E. Brunot, Houston, Tex.
Kermit J. Hebert, New Orleans, La.
Claude L. Hutchinson, Mobile, Ala.
Frank J. Jirik, Grand Forks, N.D.
Junius Marceaux, Crowley, La.
Wilmer J. Morgani, New Orleans, La.
Rosemary Pollingue, Houston, Tex.
James F. Schoen, Beltsville, Md.
L.D. Thompson, Denver, Col.
Billy K. Tipton, Stuttgart, Ark.
Donald B. Walsh, Crowley, La.

10 years

William J. Cotter, Hyattsville, Md.
Irene T. Ferrante, Portland, Ore.
Charles Lee Hunley, Independence, Mo.
Dorothy M. Lester, Baltimore, Md.
Melvin L. Parker, Houston, Tex.
Marlin B. Sanford, Sr., Mobile, Ala.
Robert G. Starling, New Orleans, La.

# AMS report

AGRICULTURAL
MARKETING
SERVICE

UNITED STATES
DEPARTMENT OF
AGRICULTURE

**AN ADMINISTRATIVE LETTER FOR AMS EMPLOYEES**

FEBRUARY 1975

## AMS Profiles

### Rafael Gonzalez:

### Webster Has A

### Word for Him

*This article was prepared by Connie Crunkleton of the Information Division, Atlanta office, and Mary Orme of the Tobacco Division, Washington, D.C.*

SAN JUAN—Webster's Dictionary describes "legend" as "a notable person whose deeds or exploits are much talked about in his own time." This description certainly fits Rafael Gonzalez, a supervisory tobacco grader for the Tobacco Division in Puerto Rico. Gonzalez is considerably more than "our man in San Juan." A native of Aibonita, Puerto Rico, he has been actively engaged in the production and marketing of tobacco for nearly 40 years and occupies a unique position in the tobacco industry of the Island.

"I enjoy my work because it's a good service to the people and the trade," says Rafael. "My main job is the inspection of tobacco, but USDA has a cooperative agreement with the Puerto Rican Department of Agriculture, so I also serve as director of their Tobacco Office, supervising and coordinating their programs."

During the marketing season, which starts in mid-February and lasts through June, Rafael supervises two USDA inspectors and 13 licensed Puerto Rican inspectors who are stationed at receiving points throughout the Island. His Commonwealth duties deal with such varied programs as production quotas, audits of tobacco dealers, insurance on crops and curing barns, and direct payments to producers. These activities have a direct impact on an industry that provides employment for almost 17,000 people and generates over $23 million in wages and $11 million in taxes for the Commonwealth.

The diversity of such a job which requires shuttling between two offices might thwart some people but Rafael thrives on the variety.

Over the years, Gonzalez has gained the friendship and respect of marketing officials, industry members, and growers in Puerto Rico. His counsel is regularly sought by groups and individuals in resolving current problems. He has represented the Division Director at annual grower cooperative meetings on several occasions.

He has a high command of the English language, enabling him to interpret and pass on to the Division details concerning program operations on this Spanish-speaking Island which otherwise would be extremely difficult to obtain. His contributions are invaluable in translating and interpreting the standards and in maintaining effective "two-.way" communications.

His supervisors are quick to point out the contributions made by Rafael: "We are indeed fortunate to have a person of Rafael's ability to handle the complex marketing situation in Puerto Rico," said Homer Taylor, Deputy Director. Taylor first hired Gonzalez in 1949 when he was in Puerto Rico to organize the inspection service there.

—Continued next page

Gonzalez (cont'd)

In 1958, Rafael was presented a Superior Performance Award *in recognition of his initiative, resourcefulness and outstanding leadership in the supervision of tobacco inspection in Puerto Rico.* In 1973, the Tobacco Marketing Association of Puerto Rico dedicated its annual meeting to him and presented him with a plaque in recognition of his contributions to the tobacco industry.

When asked, "What contributes to effective tobacco marketing in Puerto Rico?" Rafael responds without hesitation: "A dependable, unbiased tobacco grading program."

Rafael and his wife Lama live in Guayama. They have three children, Avilda, 26, Rafael, 25, and Edgardo, 21. □

# Prochaska Succeeds
# Thackrey as Information Director

Stan Prochaska

Stanley W. Prochaska, 39, who reports to Washington, D.C., March 1 as director of the Information Division, said he'll take on the assignment with the philosophy he's used over the years: "The public has a right to know."

Prochaska succeeds Franklin Thackrey, who retired Dec. 31, after 39 years of USDA service, 28 of them as Information Division director.

A native of Garfield County, Okla., Prochaska first joined the AMS Information Division as a summer intern after receiving a B.A. in agricultural journalism from Oklahoma State University in 1956. He put in two years of active duty as an Army officer, returned to Oklahoma State for an M.A. in journalism, and rejoined the AMS Information Division as a permanent member in 1959. After one year in Washington, he transferred to the Atlanta office, and was named regional director there in 1966.

Prochaska intends to keep on applying the principles he's found successful in the southeast region. "I believe strongly," he says, "in the philosophy that to have good external communications with the public—in fact more than good; excellent or outstanding!—you've got to have good internal communications, especially between the Information and program Divisions."

Toward this end, and because he doesn't "necessarily believe in continuing to do things the same way that they have been done," or that any "method of dissemination of information is sacrosanct and can't be changed," he says he will be suggesting some new approaches to disseminating information about AMS programs.

Prochaska, wife Dorothy, and the children—Michael, 18, Paul, 16, John, 14, Mary Lynn, 12, Angela, 11, and Amy, 4—will probably make their home in northern Virginia. □

Deputy Director Al Horton and Director Prochaska

## Patton Named F&V Deputy Director

David A. Patton, who has spent his career of 32 years with the Fruit and Vegetable Division's Processed Products Standardization and Inspection Branch, was appointed Deputy Director on Jan. 19.

Patton is enthusiastic about his new position, which gives him responsibility for the inspection, grading, and standardization work of the Fresh Products Standardization and Inspection (FPSI) Branch, and the Processed Products Standardization and Inspection (PPSI) Branch. He had been assistant chief of the PPSI Branch since 1973.

Patton was U.S. representative to the 1967 and 1968 Coordinating Committee for the European meetings of the Codex Alimentarius, and expects to help carry on the "considerable progress" of the last 12 years in Codex work in international standards for fruits and vegetables.

But even more important right now, Patton feels, is grading and domestic standardization work.

"Hopefully I'll be able to help stimulate more demand in standardization and grading work," he says, "by finding ways to make our grading systems more flexible and by getting our standards more in line with consumer and industry needs."

Patton got his farming start in Clarence, Ill., a village in central Illinois with a population of about 100, where his father was a grain dealer. As a school boy he worked on farms in and around Clarence during vacations. He entered the University of Illinois in 1938 with intentions of emerging an agricultural journalist, but switched majors and graduated in 1942 with a B.S. in agricultural economics.

Two months later he had accepted a $135-a-month job as an agricultural commodity grader trainee with AMS and was on his way to San Francisco.

Between 1942 and 1945 Patton learned the basics of processed products inspection work in California, Washington, and Idaho, and kept moving steadily up the promotion ladder. He was named officer-in-charge of the Boise, Idaho, office in 1945; officer-in-charge of the Yakima, Wash., office in 1947. Then it was back to Illinois as assistant regional director of the Midwest region, headquartered in Chicago, in 1952. Patton came to the PPSI Branch's Standardization Section in Washington in 1954, was promoted to head of the Inspection Section in 1960, and was named assistant branch chief in 1973.

Patton and wife Belen have three sons: David, 23, Scott, 19, and Bruce, 16. The Pattons live in Arlington, Va.                                              □

# Division News

## FRUIT AND VEGETABLE

● **John J. Dimond,** chief of the Regulatory Branch, died of a heart attack Jan. 8. Jack, as he was known, had a busy career: he started in government service with USDA in 1934, then left USDA to serve with other government agencies in Washington, D.C. He received his LLB Degree in 1941 from the Washington College of Law, and became a member of the bars for the U.S. District Court and the U.S. Court of Appeals for the District. In 1942 Dimond returned to USDA and joined the Regulatory Branch's Chicago Office. Following an appointment as officer-in-charge of the Fort Worth Office, Dimond was named chief of the Branch in 1955.

*The Packer,* a newspaper for the fruit and vegetable industry, wrote the following of Dimond in a Jan. 18 editorial: Shippers and receivers "respected his objectivity in making decisions, and his dedication to doing what he thought was right."

● **George Cammeyer,** officer-in-charge of the Florida City, Fla., Market News Office, died Jan. 10. Cammeyer was a federal-state inspector with AMS' Fresh Products Standardization and Inspection Branch from 1944-56. He joined the Market News Branch in 1956, and his reporting duties took him up and down the east coast and through the Gulf states. Cammeyer

# Division News

was named officer-in-charge of the Washington, D.C. terminal market, which he joined in 1958; of the Sanford, Fla., Office, in 1962; of the Riverhead, Long Island, Office in 1963; and of the Florida City Office in 1972.

## ● 90% Dried Prune Crop Available for Sale

The Specialty Crops Branch reports that 90 percent—or 124,200 tons—of the 1974-75 California dried prune crop is now available for sale in regular trade channels. The remaining 10 percent of the crop will be held in reserve. These figures are based on a revised crop estimate of 138,000 tons. In addition there's a 54,000-ton carryover from the 1973-74 crop year. This action is taken under a modified federal marketing order regulation announced by USDA Jan. 22.

The figures for this year contrast with a 1973-74 crop of 170,000 tons which was free of volume restrictions since the total supply was necessary to meet demand.

The 90 percent tonnage available for sale should meet expected 1974-75 trade demand and carryover requirements, according to **Bill Higgins,** chief of the Specialty Crops Branch.

## ● 73% California Raisins Allocated for Sale

The comment period on USDA's proposal to change the amount of raisins from the 1974 crop for reserve and for sale ended Jan. 17. Seventy-three percent of the crop, or 155,000 tons—20,000 to 25,000 more than in recent years—can now be sold in U.S. and other western hemisphere markets, primarily Canada. The 27 percent reserve—about 57,000 tons—can be sold in export markets.

Last October a preliminary sales allocation of 62 percent (or 133,000 tons) was announced. Although crop estimates dropped from 215,000 to 212,000 tons since that time, the Raisin Administrative Committee assessed demand conditions and recommended boosting the allocation.

An additional 22,000 tons are also being released to market. This was provided for in the preliminary allocation, once a firm estimate was made of the 1974 crop.

## ● S.S. Ilkon Dalio Brings Dates from Iran

The S.S. Ilkon Dalio arrived in New York City harbor on Christmas Day with approximately 100,000 cartons of Iranian dates on board. The Processed Products Standardization and Inspection (PPSI) Branch began sampling and inspecting the dates on Dec. 26.

## ● Roundy Speaks at Food Technology Meeting

**Clayton Roundy,** Los Angeles area office-in-charge (OIC), PPSI Branch, participated in the Nov. 20 Southern California Institute of Food Technologists food industry program. Roundy discussed the "Voluntary Program of Inspection and Grading of Foods and the AMS-FDA Agreement." The meeting was attended by 180 persons representing all phases of industry and various state and federal government agencies. *Los Angeles Times* reporter Jean Bennett covered the meeting in an article, "Food Technologists Face the Hard Facts."

## ● Meetings

**Harley Watts,** Van Wert, Ohio, area OIC, PPSI Branch, attended the Ohio Canner's Association meeting in Columbus, Dec. 5. While there Watts met individually with many processor representatives to discuss their problems and how the Branch might help to achieve solutions. During the formal sessions Dr. Wilbur Gould, executive vice-president of the Association, recognized the services provided by the Branch.

**Shelby Sevier,** officer-in-charge of the Yakima, Wash., Market News Office, met with a number of the growers and shippers who were attending the Annual Washington State Horticultural Meeting in Yakima during the week of Dec. 6. This is one way that Sevier discusses improvements in market news and keeps abreast of new developments in marketing practices without extensive travel.

**Darrell Breed,** of the Newburgh, N.Y. Market News Office, attended the Annual Convention of the Empire State Honey Producers Association in Syracuse, N.Y., on Dec. 6-7. Breed reports that the beekeepers were

# Division News

very interested in more frequent honey market news reports.

## ● Eaton Is Host to German Merchants

**Virgil Eaton,** of the Federal-State Market News Office at San Francisco, guided a group of German produce merchants through the San Francisco wholesale market Dec. 13. Eaton described fruit and vegetable markets and marketing and the functions of the Market News Service to the merchants.

## ● Field Notes

**Benton Morgan,** of the Lakeland, Fla., Market News Office, reports that cabbage marketings from Hastings are running later than normal this year. Morgan usually starts the cabbage report each year, and then turns over the responsibility to the Sanford, Fla., seasonal office in late December. With the delay in harvesting this year due to extremely dry weather, cabbage reports didn't begin until the Sanford office opened.

**Stan Call,** in charge of the Birmingham, Ala., Market News Office, appeared on a program of the Cullman Sweetpotato Growers Steering Committee on Dec. 16 at Cullman, Ala. The Steering Committee asked Call to consider starting a market news report on Alabama sweetpotatoes. Though market conditions make a report unfeasible right now, Call said, it may be possible in the future.

**Dick Koebele** and **Jim Laing,** of the Chicago Market News Office, accepted an invitation to meet Secretary Butz at the Chicago Office of the Secretary on Dec. 11. Both reporters had a short discussion with Butz who also spoke informally with a group of Chicago USDA employees.

**Doug Edwards,** in charge of the Riverhead, Long Island, N.Y., Market News Office, reports that lack of labor is holding back brussels sprout production on Long Island. Only two growers had acreage this season and one was apprehensive about getting enough labor to harvest the crop in the future. Picking brussels sprouts requires long hours of stoop labor—work that few people want.

**John O'Neil,** in charge of the Boston Market News Office, reports that the produce market continues to handle fewer Christmas trees each holiday season. The wholesale flower market, however, was heavy with holiday greens and house plants.

## ● Kaiser Pleads Guilty to Marketing Order Violation

**James E. Kaiser,** a produce handler in Gresham, Ore., pleaded guilty and was fined $300 Dec. 9 in the U.S. District Court in Portland after the Division recommended that the Justice Department prosecute him for shipping 35,700 pounds of uninspected potatoes. This violates the Federal Marketing Order for Oregon-California potatoes. Three hundred dollars is a relatively large fine for violating a potato order.

## ● USDA Suspends License of Cincinnati Firm

A routine check of a large Cincinnati produce firm, Caruso-Ciresi, Inc., by the Chicago Field Office turned into a major investigation when substantial underpayments to industry and complex relationships within the firm were uncovered, according to **John Gardner,** acting chief of the Regulatory Branch. The firm violated the Perishable Agricultural Commodities Act by failing to pay more than $14,880 to 11 shippers for 42 lots of fruits and vegetables.

Caruso-Ciresi, Inc., was in partnership with an individual, Michael A. Carlotta, who had also failed to pay an additional $7,222 to 25 shippers for 62 lots of produce.

Caruso-Ciresi, Inc., and Carlotta have since paid the $22,102 owed to their consignors, and have agreed to the order suspending their license for 45 days. Suspension started Dec. 30.

## ● Pallella Has License Revoked

After going back and forth several times with an order, an appeal, and remanding the case to the Secretary of Agriculture, a Chicago firm, Thomas D. Pallella Co., Inc., consented Dec. 17 to an order revoking its license under the PAC Act. Pallella is a

5

# Division News

broker who had collected clients' funds and appropriated them to his own use.

USDA Judicial Officer Donald Campbell had originally issued an order revoking the firm's license on Aug. 28, 1973. Pallella appealed the order, and the U.S. Court of Appeals remanded the case to the Secretary of Agriculture for an oral hearing. Before the hearing was held, though, Pallella consented to the order.

## GRAIN

### ● Southern Seedsmen Elect Rollin Member

The Southern Seedsmen's Association elected **Stan Rollin**, commissioner of the Plant Variety and Protection Office, an honorary member at its annual meeting in Houston, Tex., Dec. 1-3. Rollin was honored *for meritorious service rendered this Organization, the Seed Industry, and Agriculture.*

## LIVESTOCK

### ● The Transponder Is Coming

One day the transponder may come to the Livestock Division.

**Bob Leverette,** assistant chief of the Meat Grading Branch, was among representatives from 15 industry groups and government agencies who met in Oklahoma City, Okla., Dec. 11, to discuss this electronic identification system for livestock.

APHIS and the Atomic Energy Commission are now developing and testing the transponder. The device is designed to be implanted beneath the skin of animals to monitor body temperature and provide an information code, for transmittal to a specially developed receiver.

Once perfected and available nationwide, the transponder could be used to identify animals for the Meat Grading Branch's Beef Carcass Data Service.

### ● Abraham Discusses Beef Grading with NFO Members

**Herb Abraham** of the Standardization Branch talked beef grading with about 200 National Farmers Organization members at their annual convention in Memphis, Tenn., Dec. 2 and 3. Abraham also discussed the procedures for assuring nationally uniform application of grade standards and the current USDA beef grade proposal.

The NFO is encouraging its members to sell cattle on a carcass grade and weight basis, increasing their interest in grade application.

### ● 1974 Futures Deliveries Total

During 1974, a total of 2,928 loads of cattle and hogs was delivered and accepted by livestock market news reporters in settlement of futures contracts. Trading on the Chicago Mercantile Exchange accounted for 2,282 loads of slaughter cattle, 249 loads of feeder cattle, and 353 loads of slaughter hogs.

In addition, 43 loads of slaughter cattle were accepted for the Pacific Commodity Exchange and one load of hogs for the Mid-America Exchange. Market reporters examined each load and certified that the cattle or hogs met grade and other contract specifications.

### ● Harding, Gaither Meet with Florida Market News People

**Bruce Harding,** Market News Branch eastern area supervisor, and **James Gaither,** reporter in charge of the Thomasville, Ga., Office, met with five Florida state reporters and two state supervisors, Dec. 12-13, at Ocala, Fla. The group evaluated cattle and calves as live slaughter animals and then again as carcasses. This comparison of live and carcass grades provided an excellent opportunity to review and coordinate official grading techniques.

The market news people also studied several films on all classes of livestock and discussed livestock reporting activities in Florida. A cooperative federal-state livestock market news program has been conducted in Florida since 1939.

# Division News

Marshall Ivy, head of the Omaha Market News Office and Carmelita Malone, head clerk, update livestock market information for transmittal on the Nebraska "hotline." (Story below.)

● **Status Report: New York Federal-State Market News Program**

Four New York state reporters are now covering 17 livestock auction sales and are making 99 weekly radio broadcasts under the federal-state market news program started last July. The federal-state market reports are also published in nine daily and 10 weekly newspapers. The Washington Market News Branch provides technical supervision for the program.

● **Efficiency Up in Nebraska Telephone "Hotline" Service**

When Nebraska livestock feeders and other industry members call into the state's automatic telephone "hotline" service, they'll be finding the service more efficient and more timely, reports **Marshall Ivy.** Ivy heads the Omaha Market News Office, which disseminates livestock market information throughout the state.

# Division News

Previously, people who update the state's 15 local telephone answering devices had to call into the so-called "mother machine" in Omaha for their recorded market information. Now the Omaha market news staff updates the mother unit several times daily and the information is transmitted to the local units via remote control.

The information available to callers, on a 24-hours-a-day basis, includes prices on direct cattle sales, terminal market receipts, meat trade data, and special reports.

This "hotline" service is provided jointly by the Livestock Market News Branch, the Nebraska Livestock Feeders Association, and the Nebraska Department of Agriculture. The telephone units—owned by local county livestock feeder associations—are distributed throughout the state so most people can get the information by just dialing a local, toll-free number.

At peak periods, the units handle as many as 1,000 daily. One unit, at West Point, Neb., received 4,200 calls in one month. Additional units will soon be established in other Nebraska cities.

## POULTRY

● The Division sadly reports the death of Grader William F. **Cassidy**, Farmingdale, N.J., on Dec. 24. Cassidy had been with the Division since 1965.

● **"Egg Marketing Facts"**

*Egg Marketing Facts—Second Half 1975*, prepared by **Opie Hester**, assistant chief of the Marketing Programs Branch, and other Department economists, was released early in January. This is the first issue of *Marketing Facts* to come out on eggs. *Facts* is a series of poultry marketing reports replacing the marketing guides. In *Egg Marketing Facts*, the economists analyze the major factors affecting the production and marketing of eggs.

Among their findings: demand for eggs in July-December may be about the same as last year, with the cost of production dependent largely on the prospects and outcome of the 1975 corn and soybean crops.

According to *Egg Marketing Facts*, it's possible that the nation's laying flock on July 1 could be as much as 7 percent smaller than it was last year.

● **Hester Attends Poultry - Livestock Survey Committee Meeting**

**Opie Hester** attended the quarterly meeting of the Poultry and Livestock Survey Committee in Chicago Dec. 16-17. The Committee forecasted that broiler, egg, turkey, and pork output would be significantly lower than it was in 1974 and predicted higher beef production. Expected January-June wholesale price increases were 8 percent for eggs and about 15 percent for broilers and turkeys. Barrow and gilt prices were forecast to be up almost 26 percent and fed cattle unchanged from January-June 1974.

● **Proposed Amendments to Regulations**

Proposed amendments to the voluntary grading regulations for poultry and eggs, and the mandatory and voluntary inspection regulations for eggs and egg products were published in Jan. 9 *Federal Register*.

The amendments would clarify regulations on egg products now exempt from inspection, such as freeze-dried products, imitation products, and dietary foods prepared from inspected egg products. Under the amendments information would be provided on nutrition labeling requirements, and the exemptions for selling eggs regulated under the Egg Products Inspection Act would be tightened. The amendments would prohibit selling directly to consumers shell eggs containing more leaker or loss eggs than permitted in U.S. Consumer Grade B.

They would also change the grade standards for oven-ready (pan) raw poultry roasts. Other proposed changes are, for the most part, of an administrative or housekeeping nature.

● **Kennett Addresses NTF Meet in St. Louis**

Director **Connor Kennett** spoke on "Turkey Marketing Prospects for 1975" at the National Turkey Federation's annual meeting in St. Louis, Mo., Jan. 8-10.

# Division News

The Division's booth at the convention featured the exhibit, "Poultry and Eggs—Since 1917," and a market news teletype. Publications were available as handouts. **Frank J. Santo,** west midwest regional director, and Missouri Federal-State Supervisor **O.C. Soeldner** also represented the Division.

## TOBACCO

● **William I. Harris,** an agricultural commodity grader in Raleigh, N.C., died Nov. 1. Harris joined the Division in 1970.

## TRANSPORTATION AND WAREHOUSE

### ● Tollefson, Carithers Verify Rice Pack Data

**Harold A. Tollefson,** of the Warehouse Service Branch headquarters staff and **Bob Carithers,** a Memphis-based warehouse examiner, spent the week of Nov. 18 at several rice warehouses in Arkansas verifying pack data used by examiners in computing inventories ("Packing" is somewhat similar to the settling of the contents of a package.) With the new rice varieties being produced and the larger container bins now commonly used, there's been concern that the Branch may be computing more inventory than is actually contained in the bins.

The volume capacity, hoppering (the bottoms of the bins), obstructions (anything in the bins besides grain), etc., of certain bins had been carefully verified by Memphis examiners during recent examinations, and the warehousemen had weighed and sampled the rice into the bins just before Nov. 18. This gave Tollefson and Carithers the necessary information to make the verification. Their data, along with similar information provided by Temple examiner **Charlie Perry** on Texas rice warehouses and yet-to-be-obtained information from California rice warehousemen, should provide a sound basis for verifying the rice pack tables.

### ● Oien in Cotton Marketing Study Group

**Jerry Oien,** chief, Warehouse Service Branch, is in a study group of government and industry personnel who are analyzing the transportation and warehousing aspects of cotton marketing. This is one of eight study groups set up by the National Cotton Marketing Study Committee. The Marketing Study Committee was established by the Secretary of Agriculture in response to recent congressional hearings. The purpose of this extensive study is to detail the problems involved in moving American cotton from producer to end-user, and to make recommendations for improving the marketing system.

At the first meeting of the warehousing and transportation study group, held in Memphis, Tenn., on Dec. 3-5, problem areas were defined.

Oien reports that virtually the entire two days of the second meeting, held in Phoenix, Ariz., Jan. 29-30, were spent in trying to find solutions to a dual problem: the merchants' problem of getting timely delivery of their cotton and the warehousemen's problem of delivery demands far in excess of delivery capabilities.

The Committee agreed on a proposed solution which now goes to the appropriate people for acceptance.

The proposal's outcome should be known by the time the third meeting is held, in Dallas, Tex., in mid-March, Oien said.

## INFORMATION

### ● Premiere Held for "Behind the Grade Mark"

*Behind the Grade Mark,* a film trip behind the scenes of the food industry, made its debut Feb. 11 and Feb. 13. A cooperative effort of the AMS Fruit and Vegetable and Information Divisions, and the Motion Picture Division, Office of Communication, the film shows how fruits and vegetables are canned and frozen and how F&V processed products inspectors play a vital role in the marketing of these products.

The film is backed with an original music score by MPD's Jimmy Hall. It was edited by Bob Boyer and directed by Carl Fowler. **Martha Parris** was

# Division News

Information coordinator and script writer, and **Wes Gardner** of the Processed Products Standardization and Inspection Branch was technical adviser.

*Behind the Grade Mark* will be available for loan from land grant colleges, the five Information Division regional offices, and F&V Processed Products field offices.

# Personnel Actions

## RETIREMENTS

### Cotton

**J. Howard Phy,** supervisory agricultural commodity grader with the Grading Control Section, Memphis, Tenn., retired Dec. 31 after 34 years of service. Howard joined the Cotton Division in 1942.

### Fruit and Vegetable

Deputy Director **Fred Dunn** retired in late December with almost 33 years of service. Dunn began his USDA career as an inspector of processed fruits and vegetables in 1941, and moved through a succession of positions which took him across the U.S., to Europe, and Mexico. He was an inspector and supervisory inspector in the West Coast states and in Texas, became head of the inspection service in 1952, and chief of the Processed Products Standardization and Inspection Branch in 1962. He held that position until appointed deputy director in 1971.

As head of the U.S. Delegation to the Codex Alimentarius Commission Committees on Processed Fruits and Vegetables, Quick Frozen Foods, and Table Olives, Dunn was responsible for the U.S. taking a major role in developing international standards for processed fruits and vegetables.

**Cleone Fortney,** Chicago Office, Regulatory Branch, retired on disability Dec. 30.

**Nellie V. Griffin,** Specialty Crops Branch, retired Dec. 31 after more than 45 years of service. Nellie's service in the Division was with the Potato Division and Specialty Crops Branch. She also served as president of the USDA Travel Club.

**Willard Hines,** officer-in-charge (OIC) of the Cincinnati, Ohio, Market News Office since 1955, retired Dec. 31. Willard will remain as OIC as a re-employed annuitant until his replacement is selected.

**Pascal J. Lamarca,** OIC, Fresh Products Standardization and

Inspection Branch Office in New Orleans, La., retired Dec. 31 after 30 years of service.

**Richard W. Lawall,** budget officer, Administrative Office in Washington, retired Dec. 31 after 35 years of service.

**R.O. McHenry,** western regional director, Processed Products Standardization and Inspection (PPSI) Branch in San Francisco, Calif., retired Dec. 31 following 32 years of service.

**Vernold Miller,** Watsonville, Calif., sub-area supervisor, PPSI Branch, retired Dec. 31 after 31 years of service.

**Dower T. Mohun,** OIC, San Francisco Marketing Field Office, retired Dec. 31 with more than 34 years of service. Dower had been with the Division since 1951, and was widely recognized on the West Coast as an authority on fruit and vegetable marketing orders.

**Daniel R. Russell,** Fresno area OIC, PPSI Branch, retired Dec. 31 after 33 years of service.

**John B Wegener,** head, Technical Services Section, PPSI Branch, retired Dec. 31 after 33 years of service.

**W.D. Winn,** assistant regional director, Los Angeles Office, Regulatory Branch, retired Dec. 31.

### Livestock

**Justus "Doc" Manes,** national meat grading supervisor, retired Dec. 31, completing 32 years with the Livestock Division. He joined the Division at St. Louis, Mo., in 1942 and served as a meat grader until 1951, when he was promoted to a supervisory position at New Orleans, La. He also worked at Cincinnati, Ohio, and Chicago, Ill., before his appointment as national supervisor in 1958. "Doc" received a Departmental Superior Service Award in 1972.

**Elroy Pohle,** head of the Standardization Branch's Wool and Mohair Laboratory at Denver, Colo., retired Dec. 31, completing more than 36 years of federal service. He joined the Division at Washington in 1947 and transferred to Denver in 1951. He received a Departmental Superior Service Award in 1969.

**Ed Hulin,** reporter in charge of the South St. Paul, Minn., Livestock Market News Office since 1965, retired Dec. 31. He began working for the Division in 1945 at South St. Paul and subsequently completed assignments at Ft. Smith, Ark.; Washington, D.C.; Muncie, Ind.; Chicago, Ill.; and South St. Joseph, Mo. He transferred to South St. Paul in 1959.

**David Lorenson,** livestock and meat market reporter at Omaha, Neb., retired Dec. 31, completing almost 34 years of federal service. He joined the Division at Des Moines, Iowa, in 1945 and worked at Tulsa, Okla., Sioux Falls, S.D., and Lancaster, Pa., before he was transferred to Omaha in 1958.

**Isaac Barnett,** meat grader stationed at Clarkwood, Tex., retired Dec. 31, completing more than 38 years with the

# Personnel Actions

federal government. He joined the Meat Grading Branch in 1960 at Fort Worth, Tex., after 24 years of military service.

**David Fitzgerald,** meat grader stationed at Philadelphia, Pa., retired on disability Nov. 19. He joined the Division at Philadelphia in 1965.

**Harold Mauller,** meat grader at Columbia, Mo., retired Dec. 6 after more than 25 years of federal service. He joined the Division at National Stockyards, Mo., in 1951.

**Joseph Niccoli,** meat grader at Tolleson, Ariz., retired Dec. 31 after more than 23 years of service in the Division. His duty stations included Denver, Colo.; Albuquerque, N.M.; Escondido, Calif.; and Phoenix, Ariz.

**Mrs. Lottie Stokes,** clerk-typist at the Division's consolidated office in Chicago, Ill., retired Jan. 3 after more than 20 years of federal service. She joined the Chicago office in 1966.

## Poultry

The following employees retired from the Grading Branch in December.

**Charlie M.L. Fudge,** Council Bluffs, Iowa, with the Division since 1960.

**Morris Itzkowitz,** New York, N.Y., entered federal service in 1952 and had been with the Division since 1954.

**Jerry Leitner,** Elizabeth, N.J., with 18 years of government service, 15 years with the Division.

**Sidney A. Levitt,** Dinuba, Calif., with the Division since 1953.

**Robert W. Long,** Oakdale, Calif., with the Division 20 years.

**William L. Pirtle,** Turlock, Calif., with 24 years' federal service and 19 years with the Division.

**Nelva D. Stoltzenberg,** Lincoln, Ill., with the Division since 1965.

## Tobacco

**William C. Marshall,** agricultural commodity grader, Lexington, Ky., disability retirement, on Oct. 9. Marshall had been in federal service since 1964.

**Joe E. Tarry, Jr.,** supervisory agricultural commodity grader, retired on disability Nov. 5. Tarry had served as the assistant district supervisor, Lexington, Ky., and joined the federal service in 1940.

## WELCOME

### Fruit and Vegetable

**Peggy A. James** has transferred from the Securities and Exchange Commission to the Vegetable Branch as a clerk-stenographer.

**Philip Montgomery** of Oswego, N.Y., reported for duty at the Philadelphia, Pa., Market News Office Dec. 30, to begin training as a market news reporter. Phil is a recent graduate of Cornell University.

**Helen E. Thomas** joined the Fresh Products Standardization and Inspection Branch on Dec. 9 as secretary to the assistant branch chief and eastern regional supervisor.

## Poultry

**Eilene Cooksey,** agricultural commodity grader, Grading Branch, N. Manchester, Ind.

**Susan Johnson,** clerk-typist, Market News, Kansas City, Mo.

## Tobacco

**Ana L. Aran de Vazquez,** clerk-steno, joined the Division part time, in San Juan, P.R. on Oct. 15.

**Mary C. Giovinazzo,** who had worked at the Department of State, joined the Administrative Group as a clerk-typist on Oct. 13.

**Donald E. Smith,** clerk, Market News, Russellville, Ky., joined the Division Dec. 2.

**Regina M. Thomas,** clerk, joined the Division on a temporary appointment in Lexington, Ky., Nov. 10.

## Information

**Mary Serpe** joined the Marketing Programs Branch as a clerk-typist Jan. 13.

## RESIGNED

### Livestock

**Tommy Morris,** market news reporter in Des Moines, Iowa, transferred to P&SA in Kansas City, Jan. 5.

### Poultry

**Patricia V. Greggins,** clerk-typist, San Francisco, Calif., Grading Branch.

**Edward A. Plante,** agricultural commodity grader, Boston, Mass., Grading Branch.

### Tobacco

**Chester L. Ballew,** agricultural commodity grader (ACG), Lexington, Ky., Aug. 26.

# Personnel Actions

Lynn Jolly, ACG, Lexington, Ky., Aug. 22.

Willis Leach, ACG, Lexington, Ky., Sept. 9.

Saundra H. Patton, clerk-typist, Market News, Lexington, Ky., transferred from the Division to Veteran's Administration Hospital Nov. 10.

Donnie M. Rigdon, ACG, Raleigh, N.C., Sept. 30.

Jackie Robinson, ACG, Raleigh, N.C., Aug. 16.

## TRANSITION

### Fruit and Vegetable

Jean A. Cave was promoted and transferred from the Processed Products Standardization and Inspection Branch to the Fresh Products Standardization and Inspection Branch on Dec. 2 as secretary to the branch chief.

### Livestock - Market News

Joe McClure, officer-in-charge at National Stockyards, Ill., is transferring to the same position at South St. Paul, Minn. He is replacing Ed Hulin, who retired Dec. 31.

### Livestock - Meat Grading

Royce Chambers, Friona, Tex., to Clarkwood, Tex.
Tom Straughan, Hospers, Iowa, to Dixon, Calif.

### Poultry - Grading Branch

Gordon H. Almberg, St. Paul to Rushmore, Minn.
John H. Barker, Atlanta to Gainesville, Ga.
Otis L. Branch, Morton to Pelahatchie, Miss.
Jack H. Brownlow, Chicago, Ill., to San Francisco, Calif.
Fannie B. Jeffers, Pelahatchie to Morton, Miss.
Bobby M. Jones, Tampa to Mango, Fla.
Robert J. Kidd, Atlanta to Gainesville, Ga.
George M. McKinney, Greensboro to Ashland, Ala.
Dean Mable Murphy, Ashland to Oxford, Ala.
Christena M. Nimmo, Springfield to Monett, Mo.
Sigmund Selinger, Freehold to Lakewood, N.J.
David S. Steely, Lakewood to Freehold, N.J.

### Tobacco

Kathleen N. Billingsley, clerk, Market News, transferred from Florence, S.C., to Bowling Green, Ky.

Jennifer Brighthop, a part-time clerk-stenographer in the Washington, D.C., Administrative Group, has converted to full-time, seasonal.

Patricia B. Harrill, clerk-steno, has transferred from Paris, Ky., Area Office to Market News Office, Lexington, Ky.

## PROMOTIONS

### Cotton

Charles A. Wuenscher, a physical science technician, has been promoted to supervisory physical science technician at the Cotton Laboratory, College Station, Tex.

### Fruit and Vegetable

David A. Patton, assistant chief, Processed Products Standardization and Inspection Branch, was appointed deputy director Jan. 19.

### Livestock

Patricia Knight, formerly livestock market reporter at Sioux City, Iowa, is now officer-in-charge at National Stockyards, Ill.

Harry C. Reals, Jr., formerly in charge of the wool Market News Office at Denver, Colo., has been named head of the Standardization Branch's Wool and Mohair Laboratory at Denver. He is replacing Elroy Pohle, who retired Dec. 31.

## IN THE INTERIM

### Fruit and Vegetable

The following employees have been assigned acting positions in the Processed Products Standardization and Inspection (PPSI) Branch:

Dale C. Dunham, head, Standardization Section, is also serving as acting assistant branch chief.

James G. John is designated inspector-in-charge, San Jose, Calif., suboffice.

Robert Mogg is designated acting head, Technical Services Section.

Lee J. Virag, Fresno, Calif., area assistant officer-in-charge, is designated acting officer-in-charge.

Jacob J. Vollman, assistant western regional director, is designated acting regional director, San Francisco, Calif.

## AWARDS

### Cotton

Barbara J. Wandiok, agricultural commodity aide, Bakersfield, Calif., Classing Office, received a Special Achievement Award Jan. 8, *for continued high production in the micronaire testing operation.*

# AMS report

AGRICULTURAL
MARKETING
SERVICE

UNITED STATES
DEPARTMENT OF
AGRICULTURE

AN ADMINISTRATIVE LETTER FOR AMS EMPLOYEES                    MARCH 1975

## Personal from the Associate Administrator

The past several months have underscored for me again the professional competence of AMS PEOPLE and the wide-ranging nature of AMS PROGRAMS.

October was a month of firsts—my first European visit and my first international meeting experience. I attended sessions of the Codex Alimentarius Commission on Frozen Foods at the Food and Agriculture Organization in Rome, October 7-11, and of the International Plant Variety Protection Organization at the UN in Geneva, October 21-25. In between, Mrs. Blum and I spent 10 days touring Italy and Switzerland and celebrating our 35th wedding anniversary which coincided with the trip.

Many things impressed me. The variety of the European culture. The antiquity of Rome, with time measured in thousands of years, rather than hundreds as in this country. The art treasures of Florence . . . watery Venice . . . scenic Capri . . . terraced vineyards . . . neat Swiss farmsteads . . . the intricacies of participating in international meetings, with their language and cultural differences. And most of all, the professional stature of U.S. participation in the meetings.

Fred Dunn, F&V deputy director (now retired), led the U.S. delegation at the Frozen Foods meetings, and contributed in a major way to resolving a number of difficult problems. Stan Rollin, commissioner of the Grain Division's Plant Variety Protection Office, did the same at Geneva. The respect accorded to each by representatives of all countries was clearly evident.

While in Rome, I heard by short-wave radio the President's October 8 message to the Congress. He stated that agricultural marketing orders and other federal regulations would be reviewed "to eliminate or modify those responsible for inflated prices." When I returned, Floyd Hedlund and I

participated in such a review by an interagency task force. The general conclusion was that marketing orders have not been inflationary, but have provided a degree of stability to the production and marketing of agricultural commodities, a stability which serves the interests of both producers and consumers. In its report the task force made a number of recommendations concerning order administration which are under consideration at this writing.

The current questioning of marketing orders—based in large part on lack of public understanding—presents us with a challenge and an opportunity. Knowing the professional caliber of AMS PEOPLE involved in order administration, I am confident that this important AMS PROGRAM will continue to account for its stewardship and be adjuged a significant public interest activity. This is our goal in all AMS endeavors.

*John C. Blum*

## Director Stout: "TSD As Technically Capable As Any Group in Government"

The people of the Technical Services Division dipped into Roman antiquity to find the word they feel best explains their professional lifestyle. Rome had its triumvirate, and the Technical Services Division has its quadrumvirate. The Division believes it's coined the word, but that's the term that newly-appointed Director Larry Stout and his staff prefer. TSD has three co-equal managers under Stout in place of the usual deputy director slot. continued on page 2

Stout concedes that since his Feb. 16 appointment the term no longer literally defines TSD's organization, but explains that the spirit of working that closely together will be carried over from his Deputy Director days when the "quad" came into being.

Stout's appointment marks the real beginning of this 38-member Division. For the past year and a half TSD has been gradually coming to life, coalescing personnel, managers, and the three services that are its reason for being—management services, statistics, and automated data systems.

The staff is new, young in spirit, and eager to serve.

Says Stout, "We have the right technical expertise for the kinds of problems AMS faces . . . we're as technically and managerially capable as any group in the federal government."

Stout and his managers will have more to say about the Division's resources and what they mean for the AMS program divisions in a close look at TSD in the April *AMS REPORT*.

# Division News

## FRUIT AND VEGETABLE

### ● Conventions, Meetings, Speeches

Director **Floyd Hedlund** headed a Division delegation to the annual convention of the United Fresh Fruit and Vegetable Association at Las Vegas, Nev., during the first week of February. Hedlund chaired a meeting of the PACA-Industry Advisory Committee while others in the delegation—**Frank Betz, Jack Flanagan, John Gardner, George Goldsborough, Don Kuryloski, Ed Ross, and Fred Tuttle**—manned the Division's exhibit or participated in United's convention program.

**Dale Dunham,** acting assistant chief of the Processed Products Standardization and Inspection (PPSI) Branch, attended the 1975 National Canners Association annual convention in Chicago Jan. 26-29. Dunham co-chaired a meeting with the Wisconsin and the Northwest Food Processors Association where a proposed revision of the U.S. Standards for Grades of Canned Beets and Codex standards for carrots were discussed.

**Jim Miller,** assistant chief, Specialty Crops Branch, spoke on "Honey Marketing," at the 31st annual convention of the American Beekeeping Federation on Jan. 23 in Boise, Idaho.

On Jan. 10, **Jim Marine,** officer-in-charge of the Battle Creek, Mich., PPSI Branch area office, appeared on the program of the Michigan Canners and Freezers Association's Raw Products Conference in Lansing. Marine spoke on cherry grading and reviewed the new U.S. standards for both canned and frozen RTP (red tart pitted) cherries.

**Ed Williams,** PPSI Branch chief, attended the Northwest Canners Association meeting and the 52nd Annual Canners League Fruit and Vegetable Cutting in San Francisco Jan. 16-17. Williams also reviewed activities of the northwest PPS&I offices in Seattle, Wash., and Salem, Ore., and conferred with **Jake Vollman,** acting western regional director, in San Francisco, and officers-in-charge in the adjacent California area.

The Advisory Committee and Food Standards of Rhode Island met on Dec. 19 with **Ben Yormack,** PPS&I Portland, Maine, area officer-in-charge. Yormack recommended a number of changes and improvements in Rhode Island's purchasing specifications. Among those attending from the Advisory Committee were personnel from the procurement staff, warehouse directors, dietary services administrators, state inspectors and technicians, and coordinators of school food and dining services.

In cooperation with the New York State Department of Agriculture, **Darrell Breed,** the Newburgh, N.Y., market news reporter, manned a market news exhibit Jan. 14 at the Horticulture Show at Kerhonkson, N.Y. Breed answered questions on Federal-State reports, their preparation and timeliness.

### ● Visitors

Several California raisin industry representatives met with **Administrator Ervin Peterson** and Division members—**Director Floyd Hedlund, Chuck Brader, Bill Higgins, Bill Doyle, and Frank Grasberger**—on Jan. 28-30, to discuss marketing problems and

# Division News

operations under the raisin marketing order. A relatively large 1974 raisin crop and slow demand has resulted in declining wholesale prices and large stocks on hand.

California prune growers, packers, and the Prune Administrative Committee Manager R. W. Jewell met with **Hedlund, Brader,** and **Higgins** and FNS members Jan. 6-7 to discuss surplus removal possibilities. A large carry-in of 1973 crop prunes and a lag in shipments indicates the industry will be burdened with an even larger carry-in in 1975.

Representatives of the Hawaii State Board of Agriculture visited the Chicago wholesale flower market and nearby growers of ornamental crops in January. Reporters **Jim Laing** and **Mike Chun** in the Chicago Market News Office accompanied the Hawaiian officials and arranged for their visits.

A class of Japanese students, with their interpreter, visited **Shelby Sevier,** Yakima, Wash., market news reporter, to discuss the functions and mechanics of the Fruit and Vegetable Market News Program.

### ● Training and Education

A month-long Terminal Market Training Class for fresh fruit and vegetable inspectors was completed Jan. 31 in Chicago. The session covered commodity instructions, certificate writing, and pathology. Nineteen inspectors from across the country took the course. Two representatives from the Canadian Department of Agriculture joined the class for two weeks. ARS pathologists from Chicago joined Division members in instructing the class: from Chicago—**Frank Allard, Ernest Capouch, Jim Goodson, Bob Rosko, Lou Von Wald,** and **Keith Webster;** and from Washington—**Paul Beattie, Mike Castille, Gil Hand, Charlie Littleton,** and **Ron Wood.**

**Tom Cooper** at Nogales and **Bruce Rockey** at Yuma, Ariz., have enrolled in Spanish classes at their own expense. Cooper will especially benefit since he's in daily contact with Mexican officials in getting market news about fruits and vegetables from Mexico that cross the Nogales border.

**Jan Welch,** the ornamental crops reporter at Orlando, Fla., attended the National Tropical Foliage Short Course. Welch reports that about 1,000 growers, wholesalers, retailers, and others of the foliage industry from 38 states and six countries attended. Discussions concerned a wide range of interests including interior decorating and pesticide problems, as well as marketing and merchandising.

### ● Market News Coverage Improves

**Charlie Gore** of the Sanford, Fla., Office is arranging for the *St. Augustine Record* in Hastings and the *Daily News* in Palatka to carry reports of trading on Hastings cabbage. This is one of the most important winter cabbage production areas in the country. When local newspapers cooperate with the market news program like this, they provide reports on a much more timely basis than mail service.

A reporter from Station WHAS-TV accompanied **Les Matherly** of the Louisville, Ky., Market News Office on the Louisville wholesale fruit and vegetable market one day in January. Mr. Yudkin plans to compare terminal market prices with retail prices at chainstores on a Consumer Action program.

Having trouble with your *dieffenbachia*? Look it up in your **"Exotica"**!

According to **Bernie Schoening,** Boston market reporter, the publication, **"Exotica,"** Series No. 3, 7th edition by Alfred Byrd Graf (published by Roehrs Company, Inc., East Rutherford, N.J.), is a great help for its descriptions of exotic plants, shrubs, and small trees. "Exotica" is even thought of by some as the Bible of the houseplant world. Because of the heavy demand for ornamental plants, wholesale houses in Boston are selling as many as two or three trailer loads per week. These commodities have been added to Boston market news reports.

### ● More Imported Dates Arrive

According to **Louis Paulukonis,** the New York City area officer-in-charge, the MV (motor vessel) Nurmahal arrived in the habor Jan. 8 to unload five million pounds of dates from Iran and Iraq. The Nurmahal sailed on to Savannah, Ga., where, according to **Mark Grant,** East Point, Ga., PPSI Branch officer-in-charge, an additional eight million pounds were unloaded. Sampling and inspection of the dates took about two weeks.

### ● Florida Citrus Commission Incentive Program Begins

All packaging plants taking part in the test incentive program for school suppliers of Florida orange juice have been surveyed and approved as meeting the basic plant sanitation requirements. Contracts have been signed to begin operations. The PPSI Branch will

## • Rail Shipments Decline in January

During January, rail volume of fresh fruits and vegetables declined more than 60 percent, compared with January 1974. **Jack Saylor** and **Tom Ratliff** of the Transportation Reports Section, Market News Branch, say this reflected the rate increase by Western railroads, subsequently ruled illegal by the ICC and cancelled as of Feb. 1.

# LIVESTOCK

## • National Meat Grading Supervisors Meet

Meat Grading national supervisors and Branch officials put their emphasis on grading beef, lamb, veal, and calf carcasses according to official grade standards when they met Jan. 27-29 for a technical and management conference.

Technical meetings like this one in Omaha are held quarterly to discuss and assure accuracy and uniformity in the national application of meat grades.

National Supervisors **Lewis Foster** (Bell, Calif.), **Ed Murray** (National Stock Yards, Ill.), and **Ward Stringfellow** (Washington, D.C.), who travel extensively to keep a close watch on the nation's grading patterns, participated in the conference. Joining them were Meat Grading Branch Chief **Dave Hallett**, Assistant Chiefs **Earl Johnson** and **Bob Leverette**, and Standardization Branch Assistant Chief **Charlie Murphey**. Murphey and Johnson selected the meat carcasses for review.

## • Trainees Report To Second Field Stations

After spending 11 weeks of on-the-job training at their first field locations, the six members of the November 1974 training class participated in a program on meat acceptance service procedures on the Ohio State University campus, Columbus, Feb. 3-7.

On Feb. 10, the trainees reported to their second field stations to complete their training:

**Dennis Garton**, Omaha, Neb.; **Ann Marie Hritzak**, Chicago, Ill.; **Mark Longo**, Newark, N.J.; **Billy McCalla**, Sioux City, Iowa; **Ruby Ramirez**, Amarillo, Tex.; and **Paul Swint**, Denver, Colo. Five trainees are in meat grading, and Ramirez has been assigned to market news.

tracting specialist in the Program Analysis Group, reviewed the production of meat products purchased by USDA for donations to schools at plants in Boston, Mass., and Manchester, N.H. They surveyed processing techniques, equipment, and other technical aspects involved in producing frankfurters, ground beef, and canned beef with natural juices.

USDA meat purchases for donation to schools during the current academic year ended in early February. The purpose of Stroud's and Popp's review was to keep abreast of new equipment and techniques and to keep up with any problems that should be covered in future specifications and contract conditions.

## • NLGMA Workshop Set for May

The National Livestock Grading and Marketing Association will hold its annual workshop May 5-8 at Columbia, S.C. **Fred Williams** of the Standardization Branch, who's also executive secretary of the organization, stresses that the Association's primary purpose is to achieve uniform use and interpretation of the USDA grade standards among the states. The Association is composed of representatives from state departments of agriculture and Extension Service workers.

Williams said those coordinating the meeting hope it draws a turnout from 20-25 states. A host of Division personnel from the Market News and Standardization Branches are slated to participate in the workshop, which will include the official grading of live cattle, calves, hogs, pigs, and their carcasses.

## • Fuller on Lamb Marketing Panel

**Paul Fuller** joined five other panelists in a Q & A session on general problems in lamb marketing at the joint annual convention of the National Wool Growers Association and National Lamb Feeders Association in San Antonio, Tex., Jan. 19-22. Fuller, chief of the Market News Branch, said most questions asked him concerned how to get market information and details on which markets are reported. He said that the need for more and better market information was stressed.

Also on the panel were a university representative who discussed tele-auctions; a USDA man from the Packers & Stockyards Administration; a member of the American Lamb Council; and a market operator-producer. The sixth panelist, a meat packer, told of packers' problems getting a constant supply of lambs.

# Division News

The Market News Branch is responsible for both lamb and wool market reporting.

## POULTRY

### ● Leaflet Is "Handled With Care"

*Handled With Care—Egg Products Inspection Act,* was issued in January to provide general information on the Act. It starts out with a brief description of the Act, and includes sections on egg products, shell eggs, how compliance is assured, standards, and where to get more information. **Sheila Nelson** of the Information Division worked with **Betty Handy** and others in the Division on the leaflet, which combines and supersedes *The Egg Products Inspection Act in Brief,* and *Shell Eggs and the Egg Products Inspection Act.*

### ● Egg Grading Services Withdrawn from Happy Hen Ranches

On Feb. 15, USDA withdrew shell egg grading services from Happy Hen Egg Ranches, Inc., a shell egg packing firm in Weimar, Tex. The withdrawal will be in effect for nine months.

The firm violated the Agricultural Marketing Act of 1946 and regulations by packing and shipping eggs that hadn't been officially graded by USDA in cartons bearing the USDA grademark.

### ● Federal-State Grading Supervisors Meet

Regional and state supervisors from the Philadelphia and Chicago areas met with national supervisors Jan. 13-17.

The meeting, held in Memphis, Tenn., was also attended by many cooperating state representatives. The sessions covered administrative and techical matters concerning the Grading Branch and other Division programs.

### ● Kennett, Hester Speak At International Poultry Show

Director **Connor Kennett** gave a presentation on the Department's "Egg Marketing Facts—Second Half of 1975" and participated in a discussion of H.R. 12000, egg check-off legislation, at the annual Southeastern Poultry and Egg Association's convention in Atlanta, Ga., Jan. 26-29. **Opie Hester,** assistant chief of the Marketing Programs Branch, presented USDA's "Broiler Facts" during the Processors Open Forum.

The Division's exhibit, "AMS Serves Producers, Marketers, Consumers," and a teletype were featured in the exhibit booth and publications were distributed.

### ● "Turkey Marketing Facts"

*Turkey Marketing Facts—1975* was issued early in February. It was prepared by **Opie Hester** and other Division and Department economists to aid in the production and marketing of an adequate supply of turkeys at prices fair to both producers and consumers. This is the first in the new series of *Marketing Facts* to come out on turkeys.

The report states that, based on historical relationships and expected demand, turkey production in 1975 at the same per capita level as last year "would indicate average prices about the same as in 1974." It also notes an economy-induced change in buying habits, with consumers shifting from further-processed turkey items to the less expensive whole and cut-up turkeys.

## TRANSPORTATION AND WAREHOUSE

### ● Stepp, Schmidt Help Out in Portland Area

Warehouse Examiners **Ken Stepp** of the Memphis area and **Cecil Schmidt** of the Minneapolis area have volunteered their services temporarily in the Portland area to help out with the heavy workload there. A number of rice warehouses in the Portland area, particularly in California, have been granted licenses under the U.S. Warehouse Act, and this ups the number of required examinations.

The way the Division looks at it, this temporary duty assignment won't only benefit the Portland area, but will add to Stepp's and Schmidt's work experience.

### ● Employees Lunch on Food for Thought

The Division congratulates four ladies of the Warehouse Service Branch, National Warehouse Service Center, Prairie Village, Kan., for taking lunch-time courses offered by ASCS for self-improvement.

5

*available to women.*

*Communicating these positive accomplishments helps to advance the Department's overall EEO program, and I wanted you to know that we are aware of and appreciative of your efforts.*

● **Wright Commends "Ladies in Grading"**

*Ladies in Grading* are "young, medium, and older . . . single and married," and their specialties range "from rice to ducks."

**Martha Parris** wrote the story and obtained the pictures, with assists from the Chicago and San Francisco regional information offices, and the program divisions' grading offices.

# Personnel Actions

## RETIREMENTS

### Dairy

The following employees have retired from the offices of milk market administrators:

**Margaret Armstrong,** clerk, 31 years of service.

**Dorothy M. Carlton,** clerk, with 30 years of service.

**George S. Crary,** auditor, 26 years of service.

**Mary G. Ford,** auditor, with 20 years of service.

**Joseph H. Konop,** auditor, 18 years of service.

**Merrill W. Mills,** marketing specialist, 19 years of service.

**William H. Porter,** auditor with 32 years of service.

### Fruit and Vegetable

**Herman Greenbaun,** Processed Products Standardization and Inspection Branch, agricultural commodity grader, Winter Haven, Fla., retired on disability Jan. 23 with 14 years of federal service.

**Christine B. Smith,** clerk-typist in the Processed Products Inspection Dallas suboffice, retired Jan. 17. She has worked for PPS&I for five years.

### Grain

All of the following employees retired on Dec. 31:

**William A. Beachell** retired from the Portland, Ore., field office with more than 32 years of service.

**James W. Coddington** also retired with more than 32 years of service. He has been chief, Program Anaylsis Group in Hyattsville, Md., since 1963. Before 1963, Jim was area supervisor, Market News Branch, in New Orleans, La., for three years.

**Arthur Grabowski,** Grand Forks, N.D., retired after more than 32 years of service.

**Carleton Hanson,** Seed Branch, Minneapolis, Minn., retired after 34 years of service. Carl was officer-in-charge of the Minneapolis field office of the Seed Branch for the past 12 years.

**Warren Martin,** Wichita, Kan., field office, retired after more than 24 years of service.

**Samuel W. G. McDonald,** Greenville, Miss., retired with more than 29 years' service.

**John L. O'Brate** retired after 32 years of service. Larry has been assistant chief of the Grain Inspection Branch in Hyattsville, Md., since 1963. Before 1963 he was supervisor of the Kansas City area for two years.

# Personnel Actions

Randolph Ostlie retired after more than 38 years of service. Randy has been chairman of the Board of Appeals and Review since 1969. Before 1969 he was a board member at Beltsville, Md., and Chicago, Ill., for eight years.

Theodore Rampi, Minneapolis, Minn., retired with more than 31 years' service.

William T. Wisbeck retired after 31 years of service. Bill has been chief of the Grain Inspection Branch in Hyattsville, Md., since 1970. Before 1970 he was area supervisor at Chicago, Ill., for nine years.

### Livestock

Leonard Kavan, meat grader at Omaha, Neb., retired Feb. 18 He joined the Livestock Division at Omaha in 1951.

### Poultry

Raymond J. McMahon, agricultural commodity grader, Sioux City, Iowa, retired Jan. 4 after working for the Division since 1959.

### Personnel

Hannah K. Dowell, chief of the Employee Relations and Services Branch, retired Feb. 28 after 30 years of service with USDA. Hannah began her career in 1945 as a position classifier with the Production and Marketing Administration, Washington, D.C., and moved through a succession of assignments from New York City to Oakland, Calif. In 1962 she became personnel officer of the Western Area Administrative Division, AMS, in Berkley, Calif. With the closing of the Western Area Office in 1966 Hannah returned to Washington, D.C., as chief of the Employment and Qualifications Branch, C&MS, and in 1968 was reassigned as chief, Employee Relations and Services Branch, AMS.

## WELCOME

### Dairy

Bruce R. Becker, computer programmer, Chicago, Ill.

Laura E. Blakeslee, clerk, Waunakee, Wis.

Linda D. Carr, card punch operator, Chicago, Ill.

Marlene A. Cashwell, clerk-typist, Cockeyville, Md.

Dale A. Coonrod, clerk, Chicago, Ill.

Jeanotic Green, auditor, Chicago, Ill.

Robert L. Hoffman, auditor, Schofield, Wis.

Roger S. Neisons, marketing specialist, Dallas, Tex.

### Fruit and Vegetable

Paula Bichel, clerk-stenographer, joined the Complaints Section of the Regulatory Branch, Jan. 6.

Timothy W. Gordon, reported for work as an agricultural commodity grader for Fresh Products Inspection in Boston, Mass., on Feb. 2.

Myla Schoeneman, clerk-typist, joined the License Section of the Regulatory Branch, Jan. 20.

Charles Taylor, reported for work as an agricultural commodity grader for Fresh Products Inspection in Los Angeles, Calif., on Feb. 2.

### Grain

William Holt, Standardization Branch, food technologist, joined AMS on Nov. 10.

Frances Stave, left the General Services Administration to join the Inspection Branch, Hyattsville, Dec. 1.

Patricia Thies transferred from APHIS to the Director's Office (Training) on Nov. 18.

Timothy Thomas joined the Standardization Branch, physical science technician (Beltsville) on Nov. 10.

Dianne Turner, physical science technician, joined the Commodity Inspection Section, Testing Lab., Dec. 20. (Dianne previously worked in the same job before resigning in December 1973).

### Livestock

Ann Brandy, secretary-stenographer, joined the Standardization Branch at Washington, D.C., Feb. 2.

James Brewer, clerk-typist, began working at the consolidated office in Omaha, Neb., Jan. 20.

Linda DeCola, clerk-typist, joined the Meat Grading Branch at Washington, D.C., Jan. 19.

### Poultry

Donna L. Arsenault joined the Division as an agricultural commodity grader in Springfield, Mass., Dec. 29.

Debra Jo Winkelman, clerk-typist, joined the Grading Branch in Washington, D.C., Jan. 12.

### Administrative Services

Barbara Dyer, clerk-typist, joined the Paperwork Planning and Systems Branch, Nov. 3.

Karin Grier, management assistant, joined the Paperwork Planning and Systems Branch, Nov. 4.

Richard Hooper, realty specialist, joined the Property and Procurement Branch, Dec. 8.

Patricia Layne, mail clerk, joined the Mail and Supply Unit, Communications and Operations Branch, Dec. 16.

William D. Worsham, teletypist, joined the Leased Wire Unit, Communications and Operations Branch, Nov. 10.

## TRANSITION

### Fruit and Vegetable

George Eick, agricultural commodity grader (ACG), PPS&I Branch, transferred from Boston, Mass., to New York City, Feb. 2.

John J. Gardner, assistant chief, Regulatory Branch, has been designated acting chief, effective Jan. 9.

John Kendrick, ACG, Fresh Products Standardization and Inspection (FPSI) Branch, transferred from Savannah, Ga., to Boston, Mass., Jan. 20.

# Personnel Actions

Robert R. Martin, ACG, FPSI Branch, transferred from New York City to Savannah, Ga., Jan. 6.

Douglas Przybos, ACG, FPSI Branch, transferred from Boston, Mass., to Buffalo, N.Y., Jan. 20.

## Grain

G. Tharon Anthony, ACG, Cedar Rapids, Iowa, to field supervisor, Baltimore Field Office on Dec. 19.

Glen D. Koskinen, seed marketing specialist transferred from Montgomery, Ala., to Minneapolis Field Office on Jan. 5.

Patrica Scullion, from Financial Services Division, Hyattsville to Commodity Inspection Section, on Dec. 8.

Kenneth Swanson, Philadelphia field office to Hyattsville, Inspection Branch on Dec. 8.

## Livestock - Meat Grading

Gerald Fontenot - Dumas, Tex., to Amarillo, Tex.

Donald Kuker - Dumas, Tex., to Albuquerque, N.M.

## Poultry

Robert L. Charlton, agricultural commodity grader, was promoted and reassigned from Boston, Mass., to Newark, N.J., Jan. 5.

## Agricultural Commodity Graders - Grading Branch

Frederick R. Bestwick, Cranston, R.I., to Preston, Conn.

Grady L. Crosby, Atlanta, Ga., to Griffin, Ga.

Jessea Daniel Jr., Douglas, Ga., to Hazelhurst, Ga.

Theresa Derr, Middleboro, Maine, to Cranston, R.I.

Fred Donahou, Turlock, Calif., to Oakdale, Calif.

Dallas F. Easley, Bakersfield, Calif., to Dinuba, Calif.

Frank W. Halpin, Sycamore Ga., to Brookfield, Ga.

Charles E. Harding, New Brunswick, N.J., to Elizabeth, N.J.

Wayne A. McCarty, Douglas, Ga., to Sycamore, Ga.

Ivan I. McFall, Weimar, Tex., to Pangburn, Ark.

Joseph R. Seeds, Birmingham, Ala., to Cullman, Ala.

David S. Steely, Freehold, N.J., to Farmingdale, N.J.

Arthur J. Storbeck, Preston, Conn., to Boston, Mass.

Videlia Thompson, Mt Pleasant, Tex., to Carthage, Tex.

## PROMOTIONS

### Grain

Kenneth Bourgeois, Inspection Branch, ACG, was promoted to section head (Rice) on Dec. 22, in Hyvattsville.

Edith Christensen, Commodity Laboratory, supervisor chemist, was promoted to laboratory manager in Beltsville on Dec. 22.

Leroy Christeson, marketing specialist, was promoted in Hyattsville, to agricultural marketing grader - national coordinator, on Nov. 24.

LaVerne Herink, seed marketing specialist, was promoted to head the Enforcement Section in Hyattsville on Nov. 24.

Henry Joyce, ACG, Norfolk, Va., was promoted to national coordinator, Hyattsville on Nov. 25.

John Marshall, ACG, was promoted to national coordinator, Inspection Branch, in Hyattsville on Dec. 22.

L. D. Thompson, Grain market reporter, Denver Field Office was promoted to office-in-charge on Nov. 10.

### Livestock

Henry L. Weaver, East Point, Ga., was promoted to federal state supervisor, Trenton, N.J.

## RESIGNED

### Fruit and Vegetable

Benjamin Woods, inspector, PPSI Branch, Dawson, Ga., has joined the Environmental Protection Agency in Atlanta, Ga.

### Grain

Reginald Elmore, agricultural commodity aide, New Orleans, La., effective Nov. 22.

### Livestock

John Mosbach, meat grader at Ada, Okla., transferred to Packers & Stockyards Administration, Feb. 16.

James Pendegraft, meat grader at Sioux Falls, S.D., resigned to work for private industry, Jan. 3.

### Poultry

Delores Sands, clerk-stenographer, Grading Branch, Washington, D.C., resigned Jan. 3.

## AWARDS

### Poultry

Ashley R. Gulich, chief, Standardization Branch, received a Certificate of Merit *for outstanding performance in handling and relieving the Director of special duties connected with the XV World's Poultry Congress.*

Mildred Mussante, secretary-stenographer to the Division Director, received a Certificate of Merit *for continued excellence which has contributed greatly to the efficiency and success of the Division, especially in assisting a new Director, Deputy Director, and Secretary in assuming their new duties.*

### Administrative Services

Evelyn Muccigrosso was presented with a Certificate of Appreciation Feb. 5 *for exceptional proficiency and excellence in assisting in developing, monitoring, and evaluating the AMS directives system. You have maintained a high degree of excellent service to the Management Divisions and exercised good judgment and unrelenting effort with consistent high quality work which has contributed greatly to the analyzing, editing, clearing, and issuing of AMS directives during 1973-1974.*

# AMS report

AGRICULTURAL
MARKETING
SERVICE

UNITED STATES
DEPARTMENT OF
AGRICULTURE

AN ADMINISTRATIVE LETTER FOR AMS EMPLOYEES

APRIL 1975

## AMS Profiles

### Marjorie Mason:

### Leading the Way

### To Automation

CHICAGO—Marjorie Mason has Congressional proof that her concept of "doing the best I can" right from the start of her federal career has been rewarding to both herself and to USDA.

Majorie is the administrative officer for the Poultry Division's Grading Branch Regional Office in Chicago.

She found herself mentioned in the May 24, 1961, *Congressional Record* while working for USDA's Agricultural Stabilization and Conservation Service in Evanston, Ill. Majorie was recognized as one of the 93 recipients of USDA's Superior Service Award that year. The Award hailed her initiative and effectiveness as a card punch supervisor which led to the successful establishment and operation of one of the first USDA electronic machine operations in the east-central region.

Coordinating such a facility is not an accomplishment born of luck. Majorie had built up solid experience as a card punch operator for USDA since 1949 and as a supervisor since 1954.

Two AMS Divisions were fortunate to have Majorie as their technical consultant when they converted from manual to electronic accounting systems. Majorie joined the Livestock Division's Meat Grading Branch Office in Chicago in 1967, and earned her third USDA Certificate of Merit for *exceptional dedication, cooperation, and outstanding ability* in supervising that office's central control records unit.

Majorie describes her next AMS assignment, in the Poultry Division's Chicago Grading Office, as "one of the most challenging." When she began there in July 1971, that office was using a manual accounting system.

"Majorie came to us under trying circumstances and has done an outstanding job," says Dale Shearer, Grading Branch regional director. "Our office had to be totally converted over to the automated system as soon as possible. Majorie and staff helped us do this within six months."

The automated records system now helps Majorie. Together they keep track of 13 separate billings during the year to some 240 poultry and egg establishments for approximately $3.2

continued next page

**Mason** (cont'd.)

million for grading and inspection services provided by Shearer's personnel. Poultry and shell egg grading for quality is voluntary and egg products inspection for wholesomeness is mandatory.

In addition to keeping all those figures straight, Majorie also, in a sense, "runs the office." She, and an administrative staff of seven, watch out for all the needs (no matter how significant or trival) of this major field operations headquarters.

"I'm particularly grateful," Shearer says, "to

have such a qualified person to take care of the bulk of our administrative tasks in this 11-state region."

Majorie's sense of dedication isn't bound by office walls. Active in church and community affairs, she is a past president of the Chicago Central division of Adventure Unlimited, a Christian Scientist social-academic service group that sponsors teen activities, and has served as superintendent of Sunday School classes in her church. A native Chicagoan, Majorie says she will continue to "do the best she can" for USDA and her community.  □

# Tech Services,

# The Custom-

# Made Division

Photos by Lester Shepard

It's a Division that was made to order. First they took Larry Stout out of what was the Financial Management Division., Then they found Delores Gresham at the U.S. Army Computer Systems Command, Fort Belvoir, Va., and brought her in. Bill Thompson was a mathematical statistician with HEW's National Institute on Drug Abuse when they found him. And John Miklas crossed the river last August when he left his computer specialist job at the Pentagon to come.

They took the old Statistical Services staff, which had been under Dick Bartlett (now deputy administrator), and joined it to the old Operations Branch of the Financial Management Division and the former Automated Data Services Staff under Ken Coss.

The result is a Division that's literally of Technical Services. It's as finely tuned and geared for service as a humming new computer.

In an interview with *AMS Report*, Director Larry Stout and the three managers of his Service Groups (together they call themselves the quad) discussed their own backgrounds and what they hope the new Technical Services Division will mean for AMS.

Director Larry Stout, 30, from Lehighton, Pa., has a BS in Accounting from Bloomsburg State College, Bloomsburg, Pa. Right after college, and before earning an MS in Data Processing from George Washington University in Washington, D.C., he worked for GAO for three years as a systems accountant.

In 1970 he was hired by C&MS to make certain that Booze, Allen, and Hamilton, a private consulting firm that was designing an accounting system for C&MS, was meeting GAO requirements. Larry says this job was the turning point in his career: from this point on he moved away from accounting into systems design. He was later named assistant to the director of the Financial Services Division, and in 1973 became the deputy director of TSD.

**Q. Larry, why were statistical services, management services, and automated data systems combined under one roof, the Technical Services Division?**

A. Before the Division was created, it became apparent that the three services need each ·other. The Stat Staff needed computers in its statistical design work. Computer expertise was also necessary for data gathering. The old Automated Data Services Staff needed mathematical and statistical services for its systems designs and developmental work. So we tied these two services together with management services, three highly technical areas, for a project team approach.

**Q. What are the advantages of your team?**

A. It allows us great flexibility in planning our work. . . we shift, choose, and plan our workload. When a project comes in, the quad sits down, and decides the type of technical expertise necessary on a specific program. As the director, I can choose the best talents in each area for each job that comes in.

**Q. Do you find that most program division projects require more than one of your services?**

A. No. The majority of projects just involve one group—management consulting services, statistics, or automated data systems. But a number of projects do involve more than one group, and this is the really big pay-off.

**Q. Can you give us an example?**

A. Right now we're designing an automated quality control system for the Grain Division. Since this heavily involves the math-stat area, as well as data processing, Bill Thompson heads the project up, with people from both Delores Gresham's group and John Miklas' group on his team.

**Q. Larry, this all sounds very technical. Do you get involved in any of the basic services AMS provides to the public? Or do you more or less work on the outskirts, helping the programs to do their work?**

A. The management information systems we design, whether automated or manual, are for the program divisions to use in their day-to-day operations. Statistical plans, for one, are used in daily grading services. The Livestock Division's management reporting system, for example, is an information system they use each month in many ways—among them, to

William Thompson is the manager of TSD's Statistical Services Group. A native of Charlottsville, Va., Bill, 34, has a Ph.D. in Statistics from Virginia Polytechnic Institute and State University. Before joining AMS in October, Bill was, in a sense, working two jobs: he was a mathematical statistician with the National Institute on Drug Abuse, Addiction Research Center (a part of HEW), and was an associate professor of statistics teaching in an adjunct capacity with the University of Kentucky.

manage the Division's program, to allocate its resources, and to make reports to submit to the Department.

**·Q· Your work is very practical then. Does this pose a problem, considering the theoretical educations some of you have had?**

A. No. A personal pay-off for each of us in the Division is that we must switch book learning from the abstract to the practical. We must take the theory out of education, adapt book rules to the unique problems in AMS.

**Q. Do you think your people can do that?**

A. Yes I do.

**Q. How about you, Bill? You mentioned that in your years as an associate professor of**

3

John Miklas is the manager of the Management Services Group. He is a Chicago native. He has a BA in Management from American University in Washington, D.C., and is working on an MA in Management.

John, 35, joined the Army at 18. After 10 years of active service, including overseas tours, he left in 1969 to enter the computer field. For the past six years John has been a supervisory computer specialist in a civilian capacity with the Department of the Army at the Pentagon. His specialization is the development of management information systems.

statistics with the University of Kentucky and as a statistician with the National Institute on Drug Abuse, you published about 12 papers in journals, including medical and statistical journals.

A. Yes, throughout my career I've adapted the theoretical concepts of math-stat to solve practical problems. In fact that's one of the beauties of the whole field of math-stat—the fact that its concepts transfer so easily from one discipline to another.

**Q. What does the Stat Group do for AMS?**

A. We help the Divisions change their sampling plans for inspecting commodities to maintain the integrity of the standards. We also work with the divisions to set up and analyze experimental designs to modify the grade standards and to establish new grade standards.

Agriculture has a unique appeal for me because I've spent many years in experimental design research and I think this has its greatest application in agriculture.

**Q. Was that your chief reason for coming to AMS?**

A. That, and the opportunity to manage a group of statisticians. There's real difference between being a manager and a worker. When you have a group of very professional people under you, like I have, I feel that direction becomes more important than supervision.

**Q. Delores, you're managing two units and 17 people. How do you view that responsibility?**

A. I see my job as not just managing work, but managing people. In fact I've developed a three-year career development plan for each of my people. These plans are coordinated with the Group's mission or goal, and are working well.

**Q. What exactly are your group's responsibilities?**

A. We are AMS' automated data processing staff. We do all the ADP programming of new systems, and we maintain all of the agency's production systems, such as the AMS accrual accounting system, that are already in effect.

**Q. John, your background is in computers, yet you're not into that so heavily now.**

A. No, I wanted to get more into total management and problem solving, instead of staying just with computer applications.

**Q. What are the areas you can help AMS program divisions with?**

A. Our work breaks down into Systems and Analysis, Planning and Work Measurement, and Management Studies. We're on call to help AMS programs with needs like their automated and manual information systems, and to help them study and evaluate their management problems. The important thing for Management Services to function is to get to know the people of AMS, because the people make up the organization. We give our "clients," so to speak, alternatives to their problems, but we don't super-impose solutions on them.

4

**Q.** Larry, when all of you speak of services and clients, AMS almost sounds like a business.

**A.** I guess it's because of the voluntary grading program, which charges the user a fee, that I sometimes think of AMS as a quasi-corporative service. It may sound funny, but the one thing I like most about AMS is the pressure. AMS is unique among many government agencies and departments for its emphasis on doing an effective job while keeping costs down. I think this kind of pressure, which is similar to industry, is good for an outfit like TSD. If a project isn't cost effective, we stay away from it . . .we put our resources where the bucks are.  □

Delores Gresham manages the Computer Operations Unit and the Systems and Programming Unit which together make up the Automated Data Systems Group, headquartered in Hyattsville. She is from West Virginia. In 1949 Delores started with the Martin Marietta Corporation as a typist. In 1965 she left the Corporation as a computer specialist. She moved steadily up in data processing: first as a computer analyst with the Department of the Army; as a senior computer specialist for the state of Wisconsin, and as a project manager for a world-wide standardized Army personnel system with the U.S. Army Computer Systems Command in Virginia.

## "We Know too Much to Go Back and Pretend'

Even without a chorus of "I Am Woman," Australian singer Helen Reddy's anthem for womanhood, International Women's Year came officially to USDA March 27. AMS, in the person of Eleanor Ferris, was represented on a five-member panel, which discussed IWY's March theme, "Communications—In All Its Variety." Mrs. Ferris is chief of the Information Division's Marketing Services Branch.

The panel, moderated by USDA's Federal Women's Program Coordinator Marjory Hart, was held at noon in Jefferson Auditorium. Other panelists were Mary Galloway of APHIS, Kay Patterson of FAS, Alice Skelsey of ARS, and Shirley Wagener of COMM.

The women discussed their backgrounds, their current jobs, what they look for in prospective employees, and the opportunities for women in USDA communications. ·

Statistics show that in December 1974 there were 247 men, contrasted with 80 women, in the 1081 series, Public Information Specialist, in USDA. At the GS-9 level, there were 25 men, 11 women; at the GS-12 level, 65 men, 13 women; at the GS-14 level, 46 men, 5 women; and at the GS-15 level, 15 men and no women.

The panelists said they favor the option of part-time work for those who want it. This has traditionally been an unpopular idea, and one looked askance upon as doing the employee a favor. But Mrs. Skelsey, who for years worked as a part-timer while raising her family,  ιd Mrs. Ferris, said it's been their experience that a dedicated part-timer often works harder than some full-time employees, to fit a sizeable workload into a shortened week. Part-time work was discussed not only in the context of the working wife and mother, but as a practical and profitable option for both employer and the employee, female or male, who chooses it.

AMS was also represented at USDA's launching of International Women's Year by the Automated Data Systems Group of the Technical Services Division. The Group, under Manager Delores Gresham, prepared a poster, entitled "Computers . . . Women Using Talents for Success," which was displayed at the entrance to the Auditorium.  □

# Division News

## DAIRY

### ● Shine Named Market Administrator

**Joseph D. Shine** was named market administrator of the Middle Atlantic Federal Milk Order on March 4. Shine, who has been with the federal order program for over 17 years, replaces **Edward L. St. Clair,** who died Feb. 27

In 1963 Joe transferred from Boston to what is now the Middle Atlantic order and has been assistant market administrator there since 1970.

## FRUIT AND VEGETABLE

### ● Hedlund Delegate to Citrus Meeting in Rome

Director **Floyd F. Hedlund** was the U.S. delegate to the FAO (Food and Agriculture Organization of the United Nations) Intergovernmental Citrus Group meeting in Rome during the week of March 17.

During the session, delegates considered international approaches to the economic problems faced by citrus producing and exporting countries. They discussed and analyzed market developments in 1973/74 and 1974/75, emphasizing short term changes and their underlying causes.

They followed up analyses and discussions of the current situation, as well as a review of the supply and demand outlook in terms of changed economic conditions, with proposals for remedial action.

### ● Department Approves Raisin Export Incentive Plan

USDA has approved an incentive program to stimulate exports of natural Thompson Seedless raisins under the raisin marketing order. Once a foreign country has purchased its quota of raisins, it may purchase "bonus" tonnage at a reduced price.

### ● Market News in the "Classroom"

Marketing students have been keeping **Charlie Rannells, John O'Neil,** and **Dick Koebele** busy at their respective terminal markets.

On Feb. 24 Charlie, officer-in-charge, gave 45

students from Indiana State College of Indiana, Pa., a tour of the Pittsburgh, Pa., market.

John, who's officer-in-charge, Boston, Mass., hosted a class in agricultural economics from the University of Massachusetts in February. And Dick, Chicago, Ill., officer-in-charge, entertained a group from Kishwaukee College, Ill.

Each "tour guide" followed up his tour with a discussion of fruit and vegetable marketing and the role of market news in the marketplace.

### ● Radio Market News Dissemination Up in Lower Rio Grande

**John Engle,** officer-in-charge, Weslaco, Tex., reports that the Lower Rio Grande office is gradually increasing its market news broadcasts. With the latest additions of radio stations KBOR in Brownsville and KESI in Edinburg, the office now makes seven daily radio broadcasts (five taped, two live) and one daily TV broadcast which are carried throughout the Lower Rio Grande Valley.

### ● Market News Meetings

"Apple Marketing and Distribution of New York Products." That was **Darrell Breed's** topic Feb 19 and Feb. 20 when he spoke before the Ulster and Columbia County Cooperative Extension Service Fruit Schools in New York State. Darrell is officer-in-charge of the Newburgh, N.Y., office. Darrell said that about 150 growers attended each school, which gave him the chance to discuss market news and meet with a large number of growers.

Market News Branch Chief **Clay Ritter** and **Jack Saylor,** head, Market News Transportation Section, met with the Transportation Committee of the Society of American Florists on Feb. 19, to consider expanding the reporting of California ornamental crops to include volume of marketings. This data has been unavailable because there hasn't been a central point for collecting the information.

**George Goldsborough,** deputy director, and **Clay Ritter** met in Richmond, Va., with officials of the Virginia and North Carolina Departments of Agriculture on Feb. 18 to discuss Federal-State market news reporting in those states. North Carolina is interested in expanding the reporting of eastern North Carolina vegetables, and Virginia in expanding reporting on the Eastern Shore to include cucumbers and possibly snap beans. If volume justifies this reporting, consideration will be given to technical and funding arrangements for the work.

# Division News

## ● New Production Area for Fresh Market Mushrooms

**John Kennedy,** officer-in-charge of the St. Louis, Mo., Market News Office, reports that Castle and Cooke Foods recently started shipping fresh mushrooms to the St. Louis market from the Knaust Mushroom Farms at Valmeyer, Ill., which it bought several months ago. Although Knaust had produced mushrooms exclusively for canning for many years, Castle and Cooke plans to expand distribution of fresh mushrooms throughout the midwest and southwest as production increases.

## ● Barham's Advice on Purchase Specs Sought

On Feb. 13 Mrs. Sandy Klipstein, Wisconsin state food procurement consultant, visited **Jack Barham,** area officer-in-charge, Processed Products Standardization and Inspection (PPSI) Branch, for his technical advice on purchase specifications. Mrs. Klipstein is developing a program which, if accepted, would make uniform the purchase specifications for all 16 Wisconsin school districts. Each district now has its own specifications.

## ● Grading Demonstrations

On Feb. 18, **Ovle G. Jones,** processed products inspector at Ripon, Wis., demonstrated grading canned peas and frozen green beans for students of the Moraine Park Technical Institute at Fond du Lac, Wis. These students are members of the Food Technology class at the Institute and are preparing for quality control positions in processing plants.

**Floyd Ermer,** assistant officer-in-charge of the Battle Creek, Mich., PPSI Branch area office, and inspector **Brenda Getz** met in early February with a Food Service Purchasing class at Kalamazoo Valley Community College. Floyd discussed grading processed products and the importance of good sanitation in the food processing industry. Brenda demonstrated grading frozen apples, canned green beans, and canned asparagus.

**Bud Holland,** Hammond, La., area officer-in-charge, PPSI Branch, demonstrated grading canned green beans and canned tomatoes for the Southeastern Louisiana University home economics class Feb. 6. Bud also explained the overall work of the Branch and showed a slide series covering tomato harvesting, processing, and grading.

Inspectors **Ted Hollen** and **Howard Schutz** of the Salem, Ore., Processed Products Inspection Office, have been kept busy this winter giving grading demonstrations. Ted and Howard made presentations at Oregon State University; Clark Junior College at Vancouver, Wash.; Chemeketa Community College at Salem, Ore.; Food Service Representatives at McMinnville, Ore.; and Mt. Hood Community College at Gresham, Ore.

## ● Hedlund Meets with South African Delegation

The South African Agricultural Mission to the U.S. began its March 1-22 visit with a Monday morning (March 3) meeting with **Director Hedlund.** The purpose of the delegation's trip, which included stops in Ottowa, Canada, and in Oregon, California, Colorado, and Illinois, was to study U.S. agricultural marketing programs.

The mission included two members of Parliament and two officials of the Department of Agricultural Economics and Marketing.

In his meeting with the delegates, Hedlund discussed AMS' marketing programs with emphasis on marketing orders.

## ● Recent PACA Actions

USDA revoked the license of Ifsco, Inc., Miami Beach, Fla., Feb. 18, for willful, repeated and flagrant violations of the Perishable Agricultural Commodities (PAC) Act. The firm failed to pay more than $105,000 for produce purchased between February and August 1974.

On Feb. 22, USDA found that Johnnie Watts Produce, Jonesboro, Ga., had committed willful, repeated and flagrant violations of the PAC Act by failing to pay $204,000 to numerous shippers for produce purchased between February and July 1974. This type of finding has the same effect as license revocation: the responsibly connected individuals cannot be relicensed for two years and cannot be employed by another licensee for one year.

## ● Inspectors Busy with Chilean Fruit Imports

Inspectors from the Fresh Products Standardization and Inspection Branch offices in Baltimore, Philadelphia, and New York City will stay busy as the import season of Chilean fruit gets into full swing. Approximately 1,500,000 packages of grapes, apples and pears are expected to arrive in these ports by May 5.

# Division News

● **Growers Favor Continuing Fruit Marketing Orders**

Recent referenda on the federal marketing orders for California nectarines, pears, plums, and peaches, and Georgia peaches reveal that a large majority favor continuing these programs. For each commodity, 80 percent or more of the growers voting, representing 90 percent or more of the production, favored continuation of the program.

● **100 Reporters Attend Tampa Market News Conference**

About 100 federal and state reporters covering fruits, vegetables, and ornamental crops, gathered in Tampa, Fla., March 21-23, for the biennial National Market News Training Conference.

Chief of the Market News Branch **Clay Ritter,** who welcomed the reporters, and addressed them on "What We Hope to Accomplish Here," said that in his opinion the purpose of the weekend, "trying to find ways to do things better with the resources we have," was accomplished.

The reporters discussed mutual problems and national office policy in the interest of effective reporting.

Ritter said a highlight of the conference was the Saturday evening banquet speech by John Stiles, director of the Division of Marketing, Florida Department of Agriculture and Consumer Services.

Stiles gave the reporters his own A-B-C's for success in any field, but especially in market news reporting. "A," he said, is for attitude. "B" is barometer, how you feel about and adjust to change. "C" is creativity. "D" is dedication, and "E," enthusiasm.

Among approximately 30 speakers and workshop leaders were Phil Bradway, chief of New York Market Information who discussed "Criteria for Determining State or Federal-State Responsibility," and Don Lins, Seald-Sweet Sales, Inc., Tampa, Fla. Lins' topic was, "What Information is Essential for An Adequate F.O.B. Report."

Also attending the two-and-a-half-day conference were **Administrator Ervin Peterson** and the Directors of the Service Divisions. In a Sunday morning Q & A session the Directors stressed to the reporters that the Administrative Services, Financial Services, Personnel, and Technical Services staffs are there to serve them.

*And they came from Washington . . . attending the Tampa conference, from left to right: Stan Prochaska (director, Information Division); John Saylor (head, F&V Transportation Reports Section); Burt Hawkins (director, Administrative Services); John Reeves (director, Financial Services); Dave Vaughn (assistant chief, F&V Market News Branch); George Goldsborough (deputy director, F&V); Clay Ritter (chief, F&V Market News Branch); Administrator Ervin Peterson; Irv Thomas (director, Personnel); G.F. Pittman (head, F&V Marketing Reports Section); John Nicholas (public information specialist, Information); and Randy Torgenson (staff economist).*

# Division News

## ● Orlando Starts Reporting N.C. Ornamental Crops

The Federal-State Market News Office in Orlando, Fla., started reporting outdoor grown flowers in southeastern North Carolina on Feb. 21. A price and supply report will be released each Friday until the season ends around the first of July.

Although production in North Carolina is small compared to Florida, it's nonetheless an important source of iris and daffodils during the spring marketing season, and gladioli during the transition period after the Florida season ends and before northern states come into full production.

## GRAIN

## ● "Excellence In Management" Conference

All 33 field office supervisors of the Inspection Branch attended a three-day National Supervisory Conference in Galveston, Tex., Feb. 19-21. Supervisory personnel from Washington presented information on the new budget process, supervision of official inspection agencies, labor-management relations, U.S. Grain Standards Act regulations and rules of practice, E.E.O., safety, new training and recruiting programs, and related inspection activities.

## ● Meetings

**Director Howard Woodworth; Ed Liebe,** Standardization Branch; **Tom Lutz,** Program Analysis Group; and **George Lipscomb** and **Lloyd Brown,** of the Inspection Branch, met this winter with members of the National Dry Bean Council in Washington, D.C. Among other things the Council was interested in using color transparencies as grain grading aids, and in procedures for plant inspections. Division members plan to meet (no date has been set) with delegates from five regional bean organizations to discuss differences on the proposed changes in the bean standards and bean inspection procedures.

**Ken Swanson,** Grain Inspection Section, and **Gail Jackson,** chief, Standardization Branch, both of Hyattsville, met in Kansas City, Mo., in mid-February with two committees of the American Farm Bureau Federation.

Ken explained the overall grain inspection operations and wheat grading to the Federation's Wheat Committee. The Committee was interested in controlling garlic bulblets since wheat has been discounted recently partly because of garlic.

In Gail's meeting with the Soybean Committee he explained the present standards for soybeans and discussed possible changes in the standards.

**Dwight Lambert,** Seed Branch, addressed the Weed Science Society of America at its February meeting in Washington, D.C. He discussed the incidence of weed seed in commercial agricultural seed or crop seed. The Seed Branch, in cooperation with the seed control officials of 13 states, has been conducting a study to measure the uniformity of lots of seed being transported in interstate commerce.

Early results show that the amount of weed seed now permitted in domestic and imported agricultural and vegetable seed by federal and state seed laws can be reduced, and that more work should be done to improve and/or develop equipment that will clean weed seed from crop seed.

## ● Change in Rice Inspection Fee Structure

Hourly rates instead of volume rates for all federal rice inspections went into effect Jan. 5. A rice mill now signs a commitment for the services of an inspector on a weekly basis at a reduced hourly rate. To date 26 commitments for rice inspection personnel have been signed.

## ● New Areas of Competition for ACG's

The reduction-in-force areas of competition for GS-7 and GS-9 agricultural commodity graders (ACG's) have been changed. Taking the place of the two (northern and southern) regions that were abolished in the Division's recent reorganization, the nation is now broken down into 14 areas. Each area is comprised of one or more entire states with seven or more ACG's in this multi-state plan.

If a reduction-in-force is necessary at the GS-11 level, these ACG's compete on a nationwide, rather than a multi-state basis, while GS-5 ACG's compete on a local, or commuting, basis.

## ● New Visual Grading Aid System

Special viewers and photographic color transparencies are being distributed to the Inspection Branch field offices. To date five transparencies depicting certain quality cutoff points in wheat and barley have been developed. Plans call for producing and distributing transparencies on most or all grains within the next two years.

Designed for use at the grading table under normal light conditions, this system will eventually replace most of the Interpretive Line Samples (ILS's) now being used. ILS's use actual kernels of grain, are time-consuming and costly to produce, and are short-lived. This new system will be easier to use, more uniform, much less expensive, and will allow industry members and other interested parties to obtain sets at nominal cost.

## ● 800 Grain Inspectors Licensed - An All Time High

The total number of grain inspectors licensed under the U.S. Grain Standards Act has reached a high of 800. Approximately 500 of these inspectors will be re-examined and relicensed during 1975. Under a triennial renewal procedure, a licensee inspects and grades grain for three years, and then must renew his license through a re-examination or it will be terminated.

## ● Yamahira Meets With Hunt, Liebe

Mr. Yamahira of Kett Moisture Meter Co., Tokyo, Japan, met with **Haward Hunt** and **Ed Liebe** of the Standardization Branch to discuss moisture meter criteria, calibration, and evaluation. He left a small farm-type moisture meter for review. This meter is designed to enable farmers to monitor the moisture of their crop before and during harvest.

## ● Seed Testing To Be Expanded

The standardization of seed testing procedures and equipment is being expanded. Seed testing laboratory space at the seed lab in Beltsville is being renovated and enlarged to accommodate the standardization program. Standard seed testing procedures and standards for equipment will be developed to lessen deviations in testing results between laboratories.

# LIVESTOCK

## ● New Beef Grades: Temporary Injunction Issued

As *AMS Report* was going to press, a temporary injunction was issued in U.S. District Court, Omaha, Neb., preventing implementation of the revised grade standards for beef on April 14, as scheduled.

The following section, prepared before the injunction was issued, explains the effects the revised grades would have had after April 14.

1. The eating quality of beef in each grade will be more uniform than before.
2. The new U.S. Good grade will be more restrictive—representing a consistent quality of beef.
3. Beef in the Prime and Choice grades will have slightly less excess fat.

In addition, the revised standards are expected to have long-range benefits for consumers as well as for the cattle and beef industry. The new requirement that beef which is quality graded must also be yield graded should figure significantly in reducing the amount of excess fat on cattle and beef.

Yield grades, numbered 1 through 5, measure the amount of fat on beef carcasses. Since beef which is quality graded will now be yield graded, price incentives are expected to develop and result in increased production of meat-type cattle (thickly muscled animals with high-quality beef and little excess fat). The combination of increased production and less waste fat could result in lower retail beef prices.

During the 90 days following publication of the proposed revision in the Sept. 11, 1974, *Federal Register*, more than 4,500 comments on the proposal were received from major segments of the cattle and beef industry as well as from individual consumers and consumer groups. Many comments discussed only some of the changes proposed. When each part of the proposal was considered individually, a majority of the comments favored each separate change.

The complete text of the revised standards was published in the *Federal Register* Mar. 12.

## ● February 1975 Training Class

The eight trainees in the February 1975 training class reported to their first field stations, Mar. 10, for on-the-job training. They completed a two-week orientation program, Feb. 24-Mar. 7, held as usual on the Ohio State University campus at Columbus. Local meatpacking facilities were also used for the training sessions.

The trainees and their first field locations are: **Earl D. Hendrickson,** Omaha, Neb.; **Allen K. Henrie,** Cedar Rapids, Iowa; **Kevin S. McClain,** Kansas City, Mo.; **C. Thomas Sandau,** Chicago, Ill.; **Keith G. Schulenberg,** Amarillo, Tex.; **Evan J. Stachowicz,** Dallas, Tex.; **Jerry D. Tyler,** Denver, Colo.; and **Charles W. Wilbur,** Sioux City, Iowa.

## ● Pierce Addresses Meat Packers Association

**Director Pierce** addressed the annual convention of the Western States Meat Packers Association, Feb. 16,

# Division News

at San Francisco, Calif. His speech gave the packers "An International Picture of the Meat Industry—The View from the United States." Pierce and Meat Grading Branch **Chief Dave Hallett** also discussed the Department's proposed revision of the beef grade standards with the Association's board of directors.

## ● Feeder Pigs Under Scrutiny

**Dan Stilwell** and **Fred Williams** of the Washington Standardization Branch—plus **Don Bevan** of the Washington Market News Branch and **Bob Jorgensen**, market news western area supervisor—examined and evaluated feeder pigs at the U.S. Meat Animal Research Center at Clay Center, Neb., Jan. 28-30. The same pigs will be evaluated again at slaughter weight, and carcass data will be collected. The objective of the study is to determine whether current feeder pig grade standards need revision.

## ● Stroud Technical Advisor in Meat Photo Session

**Jim Stroud**, Standardization Branch specification specialist, lent his technical expertise to the preparation of meat cuts which were photographed for a revised edition of a popular industry publication, the National Association of Meat Purveyors' *Meat Buyers Guide*. The photo sessions were held Feb. 10-14 in San Francisco, Calif. The *Guide* is based on the Institutional Meat Purchase Specifications, prepared by the Livestock Division in cooperation with purchasing officials and meat industry personnel.

## ● Meat Grading Demonstrations

Meat Grading Branch **Chief Dave Hallett** conducted a special beef grading demonstration in Denver, Colo., for **Nancy Steorts**, Assistant to the Secretary for Consumer Affairs, and **Andrew Gasparich**, her assistant. Dave gave his demonstration Feb. 13 at various packing plants in the Denver area to show the practical application of the proposed revision of the beef grade standards.

**Jim Hodgson**, assistant to the Meat Grading Branch chief, discussed and demonstrated the proposed revised beef grade standards for the Cumberland Valley Restaurant Association, Feb. 10 at Hagerstown, Md.

## ● Williams Judges Guatemalan Steers

**Fred Williams** judged live steers and their carcasses at the 15th annual National Livestock Show at Guatemala City, Guatemala, Feb. 22-26. USDA quality and yield grades were used as the basis for placings. The objective of this yearly livestock show is to upgrade the quality of cattle in Guatemala. Fred made the trip under the auspices of FAS.

*Fred Williams, second from left (that's not including the steer), of the Washington Standardization Branch, poses with the Santa Gertrudis steer which won first prize at the Guatemala City National Livestock Show. The owner (second from right) and two livestock show employees look on.*

# Division News

## ● Veal & Calf Grading in New York

Don Bevan, Fred Williams, and five New York state reporters reviewed the application of USDA grade standards for live vealers and calves Feb. 14-15 at Utica, N.Y. They evaluated the vealers and calves first as live slaughter animals, then as carcasses, and then compared the two grades. This correlation grading—a comparison of the live grade with the carcass grade—provided an excellent opportunity to check the accuracy of grade terminology used in market reports.

The state reporters cover 17 weekly livestock auctions, with the Washington Market News Branch providing technical supervision.

## ● McFall Demonstrates Feeder Pig Grades

To acquaint livestock producers with the application of federal grade standards, Phil McFall, market news officer in charge at South St. Joseph, Mo., participated in a feeder pig seminar—including a live grading demonstration—Jan. 11 at Nixa, Mo. The feeder pig auction at Nixa recently began using USDA-certified state graders, who apply USDA grade standards. At present, 10 Missouri locations offer officially graded feeder pig auctions, an increase of two since the formal program began in July 1974.

## POULTRY

●The Division regrets to report the death of Roy N. Swearngin, agricultural commodity grader, Sedalia, Mo., on Feb. 2. Roy had been with the Division since 1957

## ● Egg Handler Fined $300 For Violating EPIA

On Jan. 27, a representative of Happy Hen Egg Ranches, Inc., Weimar, Tex., appeared before the U.S. District Court in Houston and entered a plea of guilty to three violations of the Egg Products Inspection Act. The firm had illegally removed a USDA detention tag from lots of eggs containing excess restricted eggs and had also sold restricted eggs in consumer food channels on two occasions.

This is the same firm that on Dec. 18, 1974, consented to an order denying all shell egg benefits under the Agricultural Marketing Act of 1946 for nine months beginning Feb. 15.

*Wes Sears, left, president of the Ohio Poultry Association, presents John Craven with the Ohio Poultry Association's Serviceman's Award at the Poultry Conference in Columbus, Ohio.*

## ● Industry Honors John Craven

On Feb. 21 John Craven, market news officer-in-charge, Columbus, Ohio, became the first person outside of the Ohio poultry industry to receive the Ohio Poultry Association's Service Man Award. John has been in Ohio and with USDA for the past 20 years.

The industry honored John for his dedication to his work and for the accuracy and promptness of his reports.

The inscription on the plaque reads: *For outstanding service to the poultry industry in the field of "Market Information."*

## ● Egg Research and Consumer Information Act

Secretary Butz has received the proposed check-off order prepared by the egg industry task force. The proposal was endorsed by three national trade associations, four regional organizations, and 12 groups representing 10 states. Recent Grain Division retiree Jim Coddington joined the Division on Feb. 18 and is working with the Office of the General Counsel in a detailed review of the proposal and in preparing the appropriate *Federal Register* notice. Hearing dates have been tentatively scheduled for May.

# Division News

### ● Kennett Addresses Convention

**Director Connor Kennett** discussed market news at the Pacific Egg and Poultry Association's annual meeting in Anaheim, Calif., Feb. 26-28.

The exhibit "Poultry Division Services" and a teletype were used in the Division's exhibit booth along with publications for handouts.

### ● "Broiler Marketing Facts"

*Broiler Marketing Facts—Third Quarter 1975* was issued in March. It was prepared by **Opie Hester**, assistant chief of the Marketing Programs Branch, and other Division and Department economists.

Developed quarterly, *Broiler Marketing Facts* is designed to help producers tailor production to consumer needs. It analyzes the pertinent factors, but does not recommend specific production levels.

Among its findings for Third Quarter 1975: feed costs, which account for more than two-thirds of the expense of producing ready-to-cook broilers, may be a little lower than a year earlier. Other production, processing, and marketing costs are likely to be higher.

### ● Movie Spurs Demand for Grading Services

A large chain in the northeast recently requested grading service on the eggs they purchase. Their initial interest in the program was attributed to the favorable reaction of management personnel who saw our movie, *Egg Grades . . . A Matter of Quality. Egg Grades*, released last spring, was a joint effort of the Information and Poultry Divisions, and has been very popular with both the industry and consumers.

## TRANSPORTATION AND WARE-HOUSE

### ● Licensing Peanut Warehouses

**Jerry Hudgins** of the Washington staff and **Curtis Pollard** of the Atlanta Area Office of the Warehouse Service Branch, visited a number of peanut warehouses in southern Georgia, during the week of March 17.

Jerry and Curtis have particular need for insight into the peanut warehousing industry. Right now there are large stocks of peanuts, and one of the largest peanut warehousing firms, with a line of facilities in Georgia, Alabama, Florida, and Texas, is interested in becoming licensed under the U.S. Warehouse Act.

Licensing these facilities would not only increase the Branch's workload in that area, but would necessitate certain revisions to the regulations for warehouses storing nuts. These regulations haven't been used for a number of years.

The warehousemen are also interested in licensing facilities for storing pecans.

## INFORMATION

### ● Sandy Brookover Filming in Dallas

AMS Consumer Meat Specialist **Sandy Brookover** and a Motion Picture Service camera crew went on location in Dallas, Tex., in late March to shoot a TV newsfilm on the proposed revised grades for beef.

The newsfilm describes the proposed USDA Good grade of beef and shows Dallas shoppers buying Good grade beef.

The film was scripted by **Steve Mihans** of the Information Division.

# Division News

● **New Marketing Order Publications**

The Marketing Programs Branch has prepared two fact sheets that are useful for answering general inquiries, such as those from the press, Congressional sources, and consumer interests, that begin, "What is a marketing order?" They are: *Facts About Federal Marketing Orders for Milk—In Brief*, (AMS-564), and *Facts About Federal Marketing Orders for Fruits and Vegetables—In Brief*, (AMS-563).

The Branch also helped the Fruit and Vegetable and Dairy Divisions prepare and print two revisions of more detailed marketing order publications, carrying new coordinated designs: *Marketing Orders for Fruits and Vegetables*, (PA-1095), and *Questions and Answers on Federal Milk Marketing Orders*, (AMS-559).

# Personnel Actions

## RETIREMENTS

### Dairy

Josephine C. Wilson, accountant with the S. E. Minn.-N. Iowa Milk Order retired Feb. 15 after nearly 17 years of service.

### Grain

Roy Gielen, field office supervisor, Crowley, La., retired after more than 35 years with the Inspection Branch. Roy's career began in the Crowley office. He later transferred to Houston where he served for many years as supervisor of the Rice Inspection Office. When the rice and grain inspection programs were combined, Roy served as the assistant field office supervisor in Houston until 1970 when he returned to Crowley as field office supervisor there.

On Feb. 18, **Mary Alice Parun**, clerk-typist in the New Orleans Inspection Branch field office retired after 30 years of government service. Mary Alice joined the Grain Division in 1956.

### Poultry

The following agricultural commodity graders (ACG) retired from the Grading Branch:

Marjorie M. Bair, Farmland, Ind., retired Feb. 1 after 12 years of federal service.

Henry Szetela, Newark, N.J., retired Feb. 28. Henry joined the Poultry Division in 1949.

## WELCOME

### Dairy

Vicki Auble, computer operator, Indiana Milk Order, Feb. 2.

Janice Holben, secretary, S.E. Minn.-N. Iowa Milk Order, Feb. 2.

Janet L. Hood, clerk-stenographer, Nashville Milk Order, Feb. 16.

Frank Sheckarski, assistant market administrator, Indiana Milk Order, Feb. 2.

John Vrettos, auditor (trainee), Chicago Milk Order, Feb. 24.

### Fruit and Vegetable

Sheila A. Jones, clerk-typist, transferred from Procurement Section, APHIS, to the Marketing Agreement Section, Fruit Branch, on March 3.

Bonita A. Schaeffer joined the Vegetable Branch as a clerk-typist Jan. 5.

Brenda S. Utt joined the Vegetable Branch as a clerk-typist Feb. 16.

Joan C. Stahlecker joined the License Section of the Regulatory Branch on Feb. 18 as a clerk-stenographer.

### Grain

Nona Jones joined the Market News Branch, Washington, D.C., as a stay-in-schooler. She is assisting Jean Frank, market news reporter.

Nancy Kovaleski joined the New Orleans field office of the Inspection Branch as a clerk-typist.

Janet Miskiewicz, clerk-typist, joined the Ft. Worth Inspection Branch field office, Feb. 19.

### Livestock

Sharon K. Smith, clerk-typist, joined the Market News office at Dodge City, Kan., Feb. 16.

### Poultry

James W. Coddington, assistant to director, joined the Washington staff Feb. 18 as an intermittent.

Roger S. Rappaport, clerk-typist (accounting), joined the Grading Branch, San Francisco, Calif., Feb. 3.

## RESIGNED

### Fruit and Vegetable

Sheila A. Hand, clerk-typist, Marketing Agreement Section, Fruit Branch, transferred to the Internal Revenue Service, Austin, Tex., Feb. 18.

Peggy A. James, clerk-stenographer, Vegetable Branch, resigned Feb. 25.

# Personnel Actions

## Grain

**Earl Drivon**, agricultural commodity aide, New Orleans, La., Inspection Branch.

**Beverly Matthews**, clerk-typist in the Inspection Branch, Hyattsville, Md. since 1972, transferred to Internal Revenue Service.

**Mae Parr**, administrative officer with Inspection Branch, New Orleans, La., since 1972. Mae began federal service in June 1959.

## TRANSITION

### Fruit and Vegetable

**William Norrell**, inspector, Fresh Products Standardization and Inspection Branch, from Newark, N. J., to Harrisburg, Pa.

**Thomas A. Leming**, marketing specialist, Regulatory Branch, Chicago, Ill., transferred to the Washington office March 3.

### Grain

**Jill Delfin** (formerly Jill Nydegger), clerk-typist, to agricultural marketing specialist, Program Analysis Group.

**Autrey Duhon**, ACG, Beaumont, Tex., to Crowley, La.

**J. Foerster**, ACG, to supervisory ACG, Chicago, Ill.

**Donald Grove**, ACG, Norfolk, Va., to Omaha, Neb.

**Brian McKee**, ACG, New Orleans, La., to Hyattsville, Md.

**Eldon Taylor**, librarian examiner, to plant variety examiner, Beltsville, Md.

**Virgil Wray**, supervisory ACG, Minneapolis, Minn., to Portland, Ore.

**Market News Branch Headquarters** has moved from Independence, Mo., to the South Building, Washington, D.C. The office had been located in Independence since 1968.

**Plant Variety Protection Office Examiners** and staff have moved from Hyattsville, Md., to new quarters in the National Agricultural Library in Beltsville, Md. This location provides ready access to constantly-needed crop research materials.

### Livestock

Meat Grading

**Keith Dean** - Kansas City, Mo., to Oklahoma City, Okla.

**Paul Swint** - Denver, Colo., to Bell, Calif.

Market News

**Darell Darnell** - Torrington, Wyo., to Dodge City, Kan.

**David Gonsoulin** - Amarillo, Tex., to Oklahoma City, Okla.

**Gregory Rutar** - Oklahoma City, Okla., to Torrington, Wyo.

### Poultry

Grading Branch—agricultural commodity graders:

**Gary Agron** - Topeka, Kan., to Lincoln, Neb.

**Emidio M. DiPasquo** - Worcester, Pa., to Monticello, N.Y.

**Jessie L. Herring, Jr.** - Meridian to Waco, Tex.

**William C. Holden** - Ottawa to Topeka, Kan.

**Ralph E. Prather** - Gainesville, Ga., to Derry, Pa.

**Dennis L. Renninger** - Birdsboro to Worcester, Pa.

**Linda K. Weidmaier**, clerk-typist, Des Moines, Iowa, to the U.S. Postal Service.

**Sam L. Westmoreland** - Tuscaloosa to Auburn, Ala.

### Information

**Barbara Schulke** left AMS on March 17 to join Extension Service. An AMS employee for nearly 10 years, Barbara says that she regrets leaving but looks forward to the challenge She will be secretary to Nancy Leidenfrost, deputy assistant administrator for Home Economics and eventually hopes to develop her skills and knowledge as a professional in the field of Home Ec.

## PROMOTIONS

### Dairy

**Robert F. Groene** of the Order Formulation Staff was promoted to dairy products marketing specialist, Jan. 5. He will be responsible for the federal milk order program as it relates to the marketing of milk in 10 federal milk marketing areas in the Central and Western United States.

Bob has been associated with the federal milk order program since January 1961. He was employed first as a marketing specialist trainee in the office of the Des Moines, Iowa, Milk Market Administrator. He came to Washington, D.C., in April 1962, continuing his work with federal milk orders.

### Fruit and Vegetable

**John J. Gardner**, assistant chief of the Regulatory Branch, was appointed chief on March 3. Gardner succeeds John J. Dimond, who died on Jan. 8.

Gardner, a native of Colorado, has been associated with the produce industry for more than 30 years. He received his BA degree in Agricultural Economics from Massachusetts State College in 1942 and later did graduate work at the University of Cincinnati and Xavier University. During the summers of 1939, 1940, and 1941, while still a college student, John was an inspector for the Pennsylvania Department of Agriculture. From 1942-46, he served with the U.S. Marine Corps and the U.S. Army.

After his discharge, Gardner joined USDA as a marketing specialist. He was promoted to market news reporter in the Cincinnati, Ohio office in 1948. In 1952, he transferred to the Regulatory Branch and was assigned to Washington, D.C., where he has held various positions of responsibility. In 1961, he was appointed assistant branch chief.

In 1968, John received a USDA Superior Service Award for outstanding service to the fruit and vegetable industry in the administration of the Perishable Agricultural Commodities Act.

### Grain

**Gail Jackson** was named chief of the Standardization Branch on Feb. 16. He replaces **Robert L. Albert** who is now assistant to the director. Jackson, a native of Kansas, attended Kansas State University where he earned his BS degree in Agricultural Education. He joined the Grain Inspection Branch

# Personnel Actions

as an agricultural commodity grader in 1960 in the Kansas City Field Office. From there he transferred to the Field Office in Wichita, Kan. Gail came to Hyattsville, Md., as a section head in 1967 and in 1971 he moved to Chicago, Ill., as assistant regional director.

The Inspection Branch has announced the following appointments:

**Leslie E. Malone,** formerly head of the Regulatory Section—assistant chief.

**William J. Cotter,** formerly with the Program Analysis Group—head of the Grain Inspection Section

**George Lipscomb**—head of the Commodity Inspection Section.

**E. Lloyd Brown**—unit supervisor, Commodity Inspection Section.

**Kenneth Bourgeois**—head, Rice Inspection Section.

**Tyrone Robichaux,** ACG, Inspection Branch, New Orleans, La., to field office supervisor, Philadelphia, Pa.

## Livestock

**Keith Padgett,** Livestock and meat market reporter at Columbus, Ohio, was promoted March 2 to wool market reporter/wool marketing specialist at the Wool and Mohair Laboratory in Denver, Colo. He is assuming the position formerly held by **Harry C. Reals, Jr.,** now head of the Laboratory.

## Poultry

Grading Branch—agricultural commodity graders:

**Brent W. Golding** was promoted and reassigned from Monticello, N.Y., to the Philadelphia Regional Office, Feb. 2.

**Donald K. Taylor** was promoted to assistant regional director, Chicago, Ill., Feb. 2. He was formerly the New Jersey federal-state supervisor.

## AWARDS

### Cotton

**Karen Schneweis,** agricultural commodity aide, received a Special Achievement Award *for superior performance of duties directly contributing to the efficiency of the Lamesa, Tex., Classing Office.*

### Grain

The employees pictured above, from left to right, received monetary awards for employee suggestions:

**Ken Swanson,** Inspection Branch, Hyattsville, Md., was awarded $100 for suggesting identification signs for inspection offices and equipment.

**Marian Cauble,** Inspection Branch, Beltsville, Md., was awarded $30 for suggesting the use of electric stirrers for sanitation analyses on processed grain products. Her suggestion reduces the man-hours necessary to make the analyses.

**Neil Porter,** Inspection Branch, Hyattsville, Md., was awarded $205 for suggesting a new procedure for collecting overdue accounts. He proposed a form that eliminates telephone calls to field offices and provides a record for the collection office.

### Poultry

**Robert J. Van Houten,** national market news egg products supervisor, received a USDA Certificate of Appreciation in recognition of his volunteer work with the Fairfax Organization of Christians/Jews United in Service (FOCUS). *His personal involvement and efforts serve an important and vital need in the community and reflect favorably on the Department,* the citation read.

**AMS Report** is published monthly for the employees of the Agricultural Marketing Service of the U.S. Department of Agriculture.
**Cheryl A. Palmer,** Editor, Rm. 3080-S. Ext. 447-7608
**Doris Anderson,** Editorial Assistant

# AMS report

AGRICULTURAL
MARKETING
SERVICE

UNITED STATES
DEPARTMENT OF
AGRICULTURE

AN ADMINISTRATIVE LETTER FOR AMS EMPLOYEES

MAY 1975

## AMS Profiles

### Howard Holm:

### Working A

### 12-State Beat

DES MOINES —

"There's a report of problems in Texas that you had better get down and check out. After you finish there, it would be a good idea if you wrap up that case in Minnesota."

Shirt sleeves today for Texas sun, a parka tomorrow for a northern Minnesota blizzard. Uncomfortable? . . . well, maybe, but changing and challenging when your beat takes in 12 midwestern states from the Canadian to the Mexican border.

When he's not on the road, Howard Holm works out of the Poultry Division's regional grading office in Des Moines, Iowa. Howard is one of five regulatory officers stationed throughout the country who is responsible for investigating and following up alleged violations of the Egg Products Inspection Act of 1970 and the Agricultural Marketing Act of 1946.

As a special staff assistant to a Grading Branch Regional Director, the life of the regulatory officer means being on the ready . . . to investigate alleged violations in poultry, shell egg, or egg product processing plants . . . to analyze evidence given him by various field personnel and to make his recommendations to the National Compliance Officer on the type of action to be taken against alleged violators . . . and to work closely with the Office of the General Counsel or the U.S. Attorney in preparing cases for possible prosecution.

"In this type of work you run into different situations every day," Howard says. Problems never seem to follow a timetable, so the regulatory officer must have a keen knowledge of all the programs of the Grading Branch at his instant recall.

For Howard it all began with the Crittenden Produce and Hatchery, a poultry and egg business in Tripoli, Iowa. In his school days Howard nailed covers on shell egg cases in the Crittenden Hatchery for 12 cents an hour. Once he finished school and a tour-of-duty in the Army during World War II, Howard returned to Crittenden and

continued next page

# From Personnel

Static needs and dynamic prices: just paying bills today sounds like an exercise in physics. The Personnel Division has no test tube answer to skyrocketing costs, but only a reminder that meeting financial obligations on time reflects well on the Department as your employer. Similarly, failure to meet your financial obligations brings discredit on the Department. The prohibition against garnishing federal salaries put a special obligation on you to pay your just debts. When it seems an AMS employee has failed to pay a just debt without adequate reason the Personnel Division must refer to Instruction 365-1, Aux. 4, covering the procedure for handling "Debt Complaints."

To help you avoid financial pitfalls in these inflationary times the Personnel Division offers these suggestions from the Cleveland Better Business Bureau:

1) Don't buy anything you can't afford.

2) Be sure of the people and firms you do business with. If in doubt, call the Better Business Bureau. A reputable firm does not mind being checked out.

3) Arrange financing with a financial institution whose good standing is well known.

4) Never sign any kind of paper or receipt unless it is completely filled in and you know exactly what it means. Make sure you have a copy of everything you sign.

5) If because of an unexpected emergency you cannot meet a debt obligation, notify your creditor immediately. A reputable firm will try to help you by making other arrangements for payment.

6) If you have a reputation for paying your debts, you will find creditors more willing to go along with you during an emergency. ☐

# Airwaves

TV

*Down to Earth* is a 4:25-minute farm and consumer TV feature shown in the Washington area each weekday at 6:20 a.m. on Channel 4. Each *Down to Earth* segment is sent to about 50 stations and is shown around the country during the 12 weeks following its Washington air date.

The current AMS schedule is:

**Ed Liebe,** Grain Division, discusses problems associated with moisture measurements of low test weight corn and sorghum.

**Shirley Sindelar,** Fruit and Vegetable Division, "Marketing Fresh California Plums, from Tree to Market," telecast in Washington, May 16.

## RADIO

A package of six taped 3-1/4 minute *Consumertime* segments are mailed each week from USDA to 340 radio stations across the country. Segments are aired at stations' discretion for as long as they are timely.

On the current AMS schedule are:

**Sterling Ingram,** Fruit and Vegetable Division, discusses "How to Buy Canned and Frozen Vegetables."

**Ed Garbe,** Dairy Division, discusses "Nonfat Dry Milk." ☐

---

HOLM—continued

worked up to manager of the company's hatching operations.

He left the plant to join the Poultry Division's Grading Branch in 1956. During his USDA career, Howard has worked in various poultry grading, shell egg grading, and egg products breaking and drying operations. The Division awarded him a Certificate of Merit in 1963 and again in 1970 for his outstanding work. ☐

# EXTRACURRICULARS

Sandy Elston of the Technical Services Division, who was first runner-up in the Miss USDA Contest last November, is now Miss USDA. Sandy takes over for Miss USDA Veronica Harris (APHIS) who left USDA in April.

Sandy is secretary to Delores Gresham, manager of the Automated Data Systems Group. Sandy's taking computer courses in the USDA Grad School and through the Civil Service Commission, and looks forward to entering the computer field with TSD.                                    □

The Financial Services Division team took the basketball championship in the Management Services Divisions' playoff game April 18. The score was FSD, 43 - Personnel, 37.

FSD beat the Technical Services Division in the first game of the season in March (sorry, scores can't be located).

On April 3 Personnel trounced the Administrative Services Division, 51-35. While FSD went for the championship on the evening of April 18, TSD ran over ASD in the consolation game, 50-29.

The Management Services Divisions will reportedly enter the softball and volleyball seasons soon!                                    □

# Division News

## FRUIT AND VEGETABLE

### ● Processed Products Standardization and Inspection Meetings, Grading Demonstrations

Sheldon Promisel, Rochester, N.Y., area officer-in-charge, spoke to members of the Rochester Professional Chapter of Alpha Chi Sigma Fraternity, professionals in chemistry, on March 18. Sheldon spoke on inspecting processed fruits and vegetables, and showed the film, *"Behind the Grade Mark."* He followed this up with a question and answer session.

Tom Livingston, inspector-in-charge of the Dallas, Tex., suboffice, participated in Black Education Week at the Whitney Young School of the Dallas Independent School District. Tom spoke on inspecting peanuts and peanut products. That particular day's speakers were covered in two 5-minute spots on local TV, Channel 5.

Harley Watts, Van Wert, Ohio, area officer-in-charge, was guest speaker March 2 at the Convoy Lions Club. Harley spoke on the relationship of the PPSI Branch to the food industry. The District Lions Club leader asked Harley to repeat his presentation before other area Lions Clubs.

Jim Swenson, processed products inspector in the Fayetteville area, made his annual presentation to students of the Ozark Technical and Vocational School in Ozark, Ark. Jim familiarizes the students with Branch activities each year before they graduate and enter the food processing industry.

Quinton Cummings, San Jose, Calif., sub-area supervisor, recently attended a plant sanitation workshop sponsored by the Food and Drug Administration, National Canners Association, and Canners League of California. The workshop emphasized the need for and ways of upgrading sanitation of food processing plants.

# Division News

Chuck Morrison, area officer-in-charge at Seattle, Wash., and Bill McCormick, inspector of the Seattle office, presented a three-hour course on grading processed foods for Washington state employees at Olympia. This is now a required course for all Washington state nursing home supervisors.

## ● Processed Products Annual Supervisors Workshops

Eastern and Central Regional Officers-in-Charge met in Atlanta, Ga., during the week of March 10, and Western Regional Supervisors in Stockton, Calif., the week of March 17. At both meetings the supervisors emphasized examining a large variety of problem samples and handling attribute grade standards (a new approach in grading—products are graded on a "go" or "no-go" basis rather than on score points).

## ● Dale Dunham Visits Western Region

Dale Dunham, acting assistant chief of the PPSI Branch, visited the Fresno, Calif., office during the week of March 24 to review raisin inspection procedures. Dale also visited with Frank Light at the Sun Maid plant and met informally with the Raisin Administrative Committee and Marketing Field Office personnel.

## ● Crider, Vollman Discuss Peach Standard Revisions with Industry

On March 27 Tom Crider, a standardization specialist in the PPSI Branch, Washington, D.C., and Jake Vollman, western regional director in San Francisco, Calif., met with members of the peach industry in California to review the proposed attribute standards as a means of revising the current frozen peach standards. The proposed revision is expected to be used on a trial basis for the 1975 pack as a parallel standard to determine its acceptability.

## ● Kuryloski Attends Food Processors Seminar

Don Kuryloski, chief of the Vegetable Branch, participated in a food processors management seminar March 13-14 in Rochester, N.Y. This annual meeting is co-sponsored by the Associated New York State Food Processors, Inc. and Cornell University Principal topics on the agenda this year were the energy problem and various aspects of quality control.

## ● Blood Donations Appreciated

Those who participate in the blood donor program know that their donations are important. When blood is needed it is often a matter of "life or death." An employee in the Fruit and Vegetable Division recently wrote a letter of appreciation for the blood received by her mother through the program. We want to share this letter with you:

*Members of the Agriculture Blood Donor Group*

*ATTENTION: Miss Elizabeth Gallagher*

*I want to thank you and say how much I appreciate your supplying blood for my Mother, Edith Ambrogi, while she was ill in the hospital recently.*

*We are happy she is now recuperating at home and are grateful to each and everyone who is involved in this wonderful program.*

*Most sincerely,*

*Catherine Ambrogi*

## ● Hand Attends Meeting to Discuss Standards for Grades of Potatoes for Chipping

Gil Hand, Standardization Section, Fresh Products Standardization and Inspection Branch, attended a meeting co-sponsored by the Potato Chip International Institute and the Red River Valley Potato Growers Association at Grand Forks, N.D., on March 16. The purpose of the meeting was to explain the study draft to consider issuing U.S. Standards for Grades of Potatoes for Chipping.

## ● First Standards Developed for Mechanically Harvested Commodity

New U.S. Standards for Grades of Mechanically Harvested American (Eastern Type) Grapes for Processing and Freezing were published in the *Federal Register* on April 4, and become effective May 15. The standards would establish minimum soluble solids requirements

# Division News

as well as requirements limiting decay and other quality and condition factors and foreign material. These are the first grade standards developed specifically for a mechanically harvested commodity.

## ● Market News Visitors

Bill McCauley, officer-in-charge, Dallas, Tex., was visited in mid-March by Eleazar Davila, assistant trade commissioner of the Mexican Trade Commission, who was particularly interested in packaging fresh fruits and vegetables.

Fernando Vega, the Mexican consul, visited Tom Cooper, officer-in-charge, Nogales, Ariz., in early March to obtain statistics on the volume of produce entering the U.S. through the Port of Nogales, as well as data from which he could compute the produce value.

The Irish Trade Office at Los Angeles asked the Nogales, Ariz., Market News Office for information on tomato import restrictions, prices, destinations, and volume. According to Tom Cooper, Ireland is considering exporting tomatoes to the U.S.

John E. Noel, assistant attorney general for the state of Illinois, visited Dick Koebele, officer-in-charge, Chicago, Ill., in early March. The state does considerable institutional buying and Noel wanted to become more familiar with the way business is conducted at the wholesale level and the use of market news reports.

Senator Walter Huddleston of Kentucky, chairman of the Agricultural Subcommittee on Food Costs, visited the Louisville produce terminal in early March to learn where the profit goes on fruits and vegetables and other foods. He questioned reporter Les Matherly about all phases of the program, especially shipping point and wholesale prices and who uses market news reports.

Tom Hill and Bill Crocker, New York, N.Y., continue to conduct tours of the Hunts Point Market for foreign visitors. When Domingo Marte, secretaria de agricultura Santo Domingo, Dominican Republic, and Jose Compres of the Dominican Republic Export Promotion Center of New York City, visited the Market on March 17, they were primarily interested in shipping avocados, mangoes, limes, papayas and pineapples from the Dominican Republic to the U.S.

Joaquin Villanueva Llano, oficial mayor de la H. Alcaldia Municipal of La Paz, Bolivia, Clovis Villegas Panoso, and Jairo M. Hinestrosia, director of the Cavasa Company, Cali, Colombia, visited the Market with their interpreter, Liliana Milani, on March 19.

They were interested in getting firsthand knowledge of the physical layout and operation of a large fruit and vegetable market. Tom and Bill explained market news reports and their function in the marketplace to all their guests.

## ● Rannells Gives Market Tour

Charlie Rannells, officer-in-charge, Pittsburgh, Pa., took a group of nine students from the University of Pittsburgh Graduate School of Public and International Affairs on a tour of the produce market in early March; Charlie discussed produce marketing and the function of market news.

## ● Johnson Reports Higher California Truck Rates

Max Johnson, chief of the Sacremento, Calif., Federal-State Market News Office, reports that the Public Utilities Commission in California has approved a doubling of the surcharge, from 5 to 10 percent, to truckers on mileage rates within California.

## ● Long Island Grows New Potato

Doug Edwards, officer-in-charge, Riverhead, Long Island, N.Y., Market News Office, reports that Long Island is growing a new potato variety, the Hudson. It is a Round White potato which is nematode (worm) resistant, unlike the Superior and Katahdin varieties which make up the bulk of Long Island shipments. The nematode remains a serious problem on Long Island.

## ● Maine Moves Culls for Stock Feed

According to John Boyle, officer-in-charge, Presque Isle, Maine, Market News Office, the Maine Department of Agriculture is issuing permits for the movement of cull potatoes for use as stock feed this year. Cull potatoes are out of grade, and in other years are moved to processors. Because potato stocks are so heavy this year, though, processors don't want them. Most of the cull potatoes are being sold within the state, but some are being shipped to Massachusetts, New Hampshire, and Vermont.

## ● Price Arbitrating $2 Million Maine Dispute

Since mid-March Mike Price, head of the Regulatory's Branch's Complaint Section, has been arbitrating a dispute involving almost $2 million between a Maine potato processor and 70 Maine potato growers (represented by the Agricultural Bargaining Council and the Maine Potato Council).

# Division News

Mike explains that the negotiations, which are still not completely settled, are "emotional on both sides." The processor had a disastrous fire early in the 1974-75 season, but after his contracts for potatoes for processing were settled. The question under dispute is: is the processor obligated to take the balance of the contracted-for deliveries, which he can't fully handle or pay for, or does the "act of God" clause in the contract release him from further obligation? The processor said he would be forced into bankruptcy if not excused from further liability; but many small growers would be put out of business if the contract is dismissed.

Mike said that as of this writing a majority of the growers have voted to accept a pro-rata delivery contract offered by the processor: the chief terms of the proposed settlement are that the processor would take 65% of the tonnage contracted for under the 1974-75 contract.

## ● Zambito Negotiates $50,000 Massachusetts Settlement

**Charles Zambito**, a representative of the Northeastern Regional Field Office, Regulatory Branch, has negotiated a $50,000 informal settlement under highly complex circumstances, between a Massachusetts retail grocery chain and a large Boston wholesaler. The parties had entered into a complicated contract involving the sale of produce, trucking, and profit margins. The wholesaler claimed that the buyer owed $102,000 for goods purchased, and the parties and their lawyers disputed the matter into a deadlock. Chuck sat down with the parties and their lawyers, arranged an equitable settlement, and obtained payment for the wholesaler.

## ● Training Sessions for Regulatory Employees

The Regulatory Branch is holding training sessions to familiarize its employees with other areas of Division work. Attending an orientation session on Fresh Products Standardization and Inspection activities, conducted by **Charlie Littleton** were: **Tom Leming, Lucy Montgillion, Norm Riddle, Harold Rosenberg, and Glenn Turnbow**. Attending a PPSI meeting conducted by **Charlie Luxford** and **Joe Fly** were: **Tom Leming, Lucy Montgillion, Norm Riddle, and Floyd White**.

## GRAIN

## ● Record Loading of Corn at Norfolk

Two million bushels of corn were loaded aboard a ship at Norfolk, Va., in March, an amount exceeded only once before in Norfolk.

## ● Blizzard Halts Grain Operations

The worst blizzard in 30 years halted all grain operations in the Duluth-Superior area on March 24. Waves over 20 feet and 103-miles-per-hour winds were recorded. Only snowmobile and ski transportation was available.

## ● Licenses Suspended

The licenses of five grain inspectors employed by the Houston Merchant Exchange, a private inspection agency, were suspended March 28. The five inspectors were indicted by a federal grand jury in Houston, Tex., for allegedly accepting bribes between 1970 and 1974 to make improper official stowage examinations (inspectors make these examinations to certify that ships' holds are in proper condition to receive grain).

## ● Field Notes

**Vera Colbry**, officer-in-charge of the Sacramento, Calif., Seed Branch Field Office, traveled to Modesto in March to investigate complaints of violations under the Federal Seed Act, and to attend the annual meeting of the California Seed Association. Vera said that seedsmen at the meeting were interested in discussing the interstate and import provisions of the Act.

**Jim Effenberger**, seed technologist, worked March 9 to 14 in the Oregon State University seed laboratory to broaden his knowledge of seed testing techniques. Jim also attended a three-day Seedsmen's Short Course, where he met officials and seedsmen from Oregon and Washington, and observed new techniques for blending and processing seed.

**Doris Baxter**, seed technologist, attended a meeting of Western Seed Analysts in Pullman, Wash., March 17 to 22. Doris discussed the work being done to solve current problems in seed testing, and briefed analysts on the Seed Branch's program to standardize testing techniques.

## ● Seed Imports Up

By the end of March, 60 million pounds of agricultural seed had been imported, in contrast to just under 35 million pounds for the same period in the last fiscal year. Accounting for part of the increase was corn seed, up from over 5 million to over 15 million pounds, and wheat seed, up from 2.5 million to 10.6 million pounds—the big increase being 8.2 million pounds from Mexico. Import actions (of seed lots) were up nearly 20 percent over a year ago.

# Division News

## ● Japanese Officials Visit PVP Office

From March 27 to April 3, three Japanese officials visited the Plant Variety Protection Office to discuss with **Stan Rollin**, commissioner, and **Bernard Leese**, chief examiner, the procedures used to examine and search applications and grant certificates under the Plant Variety Protection Act. The officials will recommend a variety protection law for Japan.

## ● Edwards, Rollin Speak with Seed Certification Advisors

**Clyde Edwards**, chief, Seed Branch, and **Stan Rollin**, spoke with the Advisory and Executive Committees of the Association of Official Seed Certifying Agencies in Phoenix, Ariz., March 20 and 21. State certification agencies administer the certified seed programs in producing, processing, and labeling pedigreed seed. Clyde gave Association members information on the new regulations of the Federal Seed Act, which establish minimum standards and procedures for certifying agencies.

## ● Edwards Participates in Seedmen's Short Course

**Clyde Edwards** presented a paper at the Seedsmen's Short Course sponsored by Oregon State University at Corvallis, March 11 and 12. Clyde said the seedsmen were interested in the correct procedures for keeping proper records for shipping seed subject to the Federal Seed Act.

## ● Cotter, Gallup Active in GEAPS Convention

**Jerry Cotter**, head, Grain Inspection Section, Inspection Branch, and **Dick Gallup**, industrial specialist, Standardization Branch, were among 1,000 attendees at the 46th Technical Conference of the Grain Elevators and Processors Society, March 9 to 12. Jerry, along with Max Spencer of Continental Grain, Henry Kaufmann of Cargill, and Ron Murphy of Mid-States Terminal, was on a panel that discussed the Grain Division's shiploading plans. Jerry presented the history, development, and concept of Plan A, a statistical plan for grading grain being loaded aboard ships, and Spencer and Kaufmann then gave the industry's view: Spencer opposed Plan A for elevators without shipping bins, but Kaufmann favored it.

Dick Gallup described the new visual aid grading system, which uses color tranparencies of grain rather than the actual kernels.

## ● Division Reps to Iowa Grain Inspectors' Meeting

**John Marshall** and **J. T. Abshier**, Inspection Branch, were guest speakers at the Iowa Grain Inspectors' Association Meeting at Davenport, March 8. Field office supervisors of the Inspection Branch, **Belmer Ekis** (Des Moines), and **John Cosby** (Cedar Rapids), also attended, along with **Norris Davidson**, agricultural commodity grader from Cedar Rapids. John Marshall described changes in the organization of the Division; changes in the standards for grain; improved supervision plans of official inspection agencies; and proposed inspection plans for unit trains. Association members were very interested in the proposed tolerances for grading grain being loaded on unit trains.

J.T. explained the designation of official inspection areas, and the proposed amendments of the regulations under the U.S. Grain Standards Act.

## LIVESTOCK

● **Frank J. Fenton**, meat grader stationed at New Orleans, La., died Feb. 23. Frank joined the meat grading service at New Orleans in 1951. He worked at West Point and Tupelo, Miss., before being reassigned to New Orleans in 1969.

*Livestock market reporter Darell Darnell (left) receives a plaque in recognition of his assistance to the Future Farmers of America program in Wyoming. The Torrington, Wyo., Trailblazer chapter president presents the award on behalf of the state association.*  ▶

# Division News

## ● Darnell Honored by FFA

**Darell Darnell**, livestock market reporter now stationed at Dodge City, Kan., and formerly at Torrington, Wyo., was honored Feb. 13 by the Wyoming State Association of the Future Farmers of America (FFA) for outstanding service to the FFA program in Wyoming. During his assignment in Wyoming (August 1971 - February 1975), Darell worked with FFA chapters throughout the state, instructing the students in federal grades for both livestock and meat. In 1974, he was awarded the honorary chapter farmer degree by the Torrington, Wyo., FFA chapter. He was transferred to Dodge City Feb. 16.

## ● Reporters Meet in Arkansas & Kentucky

Federal-State reporter conferences were held in Arkansas and Kentucky during March. **Bruce Harding**, Market News Branch eastern area supervisor, attended both meetings. **Tom Cox**, head of the market news office in Louisville, hosted the Kentucky conference, March 27-28, which was attended by eight state reporters. Attending the meeting at Little Rock, Ark., were **Bill Fulton**, officer-in-charge at that location, **James Clower** of the University of Arkansas Extension Service (a former Market News Branch employee), and five state reporters.

The purpose of both conferences was to review USDA live grade standards for cattle, feeder pigs, and hogs to insure uniform federal grade application. The state reporters cover livestock auctions for market news reports under Federal-State programs.

## ● Market News Officials Discuss Services at Industry Meetings

**Ron Boyd**, market news officer-in-charge at Salt Lake City, Utah, discussed Livestock Division responsibility in the delivery of feeder cattle on futures contracts at each of three annual Idaho Bankers' Association Agricultural Forums, March 24-26. The meetings were held at three locations—Lewiston, Boise, and Pocatello—to reach as many people as possible. Ron explained that, when requested by a commodity exchange, market reporters examine each load of cattle delivered to settle futures contracts and certify that the cattle meet grade and other contract specifications.

**Bob Jorgensen**, market news western area supervisor, and **Marshall Ivy**, head of the market news office at Omaha, Neb, were featured on the program of the First National Bank of Omaha's 10th Annual Wagon Roundup at the Ak-Sar-Ben Pavillion. They discussed and demonstrated the mechanics of delivering and receiving a load of slaughter cattle in settlement of a futures contract. Thirteen head of cattle were used to demonstrate both acceptable and unacceptable animals. More than 1200 bankers, cattle feeders, and other industry members attended the Roundup.

**Bill Fulton**, market news officer-in-charge at Little Rock, Ark., discussed, and used slides to demonstrate, USDA slaughter cattle grades at a meeting of Washington County, Ark., beef producers during the last week in February. He also showed a film on feeder cattle grades. About 150 people attended the meeting.

Earlier in the year, on Feb. 11-14, **Bob Jorgensen** had participated in a marketing information panel at the Iowa Cattle Feeders meeting, Des Moines. Bob discussed the collection and dissemination of livestock market news information. About 1000 people attended this meeting.

# POULTRY

## ● Kennett Visits with Turkey Producers

In mid-March, **Director Connor Kennett** updated the *Turkey Marketing Facts—1975* at a Northeastern Poultry Producers Council (NEPPCO) meeting. The meeting was held in Gettysburg, Pa., and was one of NEPPCO's periodic conferences for turkey raisers.

## ● Egg Research and Consumer Information Act

As indicated in the April *AMS Report*, **Secretary Butz** received a proposed egg checkoff order prepared by the industry task force.

Hearings have been scheduled for this month—beginning May 6 in Atlanta and continuing in Philadelphia, Des Moines, Dallas, and San Francisco.

The purpose of the hearings is to compile evidence on the need for a national egg research and promotion program, to determine whether the proposed order would be adequate, and to publicly examine all the provisions of the proposal.

The proposal provides for a nationally coordinated research and consumer information program to be financed by a producer assessment of up to 5 cents per 30-dozen case of eggs handled. Producers having more than 3,000 laying hens would be assessed, but those not wishing to participate would receive refunds upon request.

The proposed order exempts from assessment producers with 3,000 or fewer laying hens and owners of breeding hen flocks, if eggs are produced primarily for hatching baby chicks.

# Division News

If sufficient evidence is developed at the hearings to support the proposal—or appropriate revisions of it—and it is approved by the Secretary of Agriculture, the proposed order will be voted on by producers in a national referendum.

The order would become effective only if favored by at least two-thirds of the producers voting, or by a simple majority of producers voting if they account for at least two-thirds of the commercial eggs represented in the referendum.

**Oscar Elder** of the Information Division, Washington, D.C., will attend all of the hearings. He and a representative from each Information Regional office will handle media liaison services in each city.

## TRANSPORTATION AND WAREHOUSE

### ● Computerized Record-Keeping

**Rolland Hendricks** of the Prairie Village National Warehouse Service Center and **Bill Rausch** of the Omaha Area Office of the Warehouse Service Branch, attended a three-day conference, called by the Far-Mar Co., in April in Hutchinson, Kan. The Far-Mar Co., a grain cooperative, has designed a new system to handle the wide variety of reports it must keep from its many warehouses.

Far-Mar is licensed, and its records are, therefore, audited, under the U.S. Warehouse Act. Rolland and Bill were called in to make certain that the Company's new system, the data processing of grain accounting by computer printouts, fills the record-keeping requirements of the Act.

Besides the fact that records are a vital part of warehouse examinations, the matter is of particular interest to the Branch because an increasing number of companies are turning to computers for record purposes.

At the conference, which was attended by a cross-section of people concerned with grain storage, Bill and Rolland explained the record requirements for completing an examination. They concluded that the system under study by Far-Mar is superior to most other systems in use, especially those in the Minneapolis area.

When actual examinations are made at the Far-Mar grain warehouses where the Company is installing its new system, more definite conclusions will be drawn about the suitability of computerized record-keeping by Warehouse Act licensees for our purposes.

### ● USDA Club Honors Warehouse Service Center

The USDA Club of Greater Kansas City, honored the National Warehouse Service Center of the Warehouse Service Branch as the March "Office of the Month". A presentation was made to Officer-in-Charge **Don Hodges** on behalf of the entire staff at the Club's monthly luncheon meeting. Those present heard a talk on the history, present status, and future plans of the Agricultural Hall of Fame at Bonner Springs, Kan.

### ● "Terrible Week That Was"

The Minneapolis office of the Warehouse Service Branch describes the week of March 24 as "the terrible week that was." Two separate blizzards hit the area with snowfalls that brought activity to a standstill. Work reports show that 432 man-hours of productive time was lost.

When severe weather makes news in the Minneapolis area, one should be willing to accept it as indeed bad.

## INFORMATION

### ● "The Connecting Link"

An 8-9 minute narrated feature movie, *The Connecting Link*, on the Livestock Division's Beef Carcass Data Service, was completed in April.

**Steve Mihans** of the Information Division, who worked on the film, describes it as "a very practical, how-to movie." *The Connecting Link* explains the purpose of the Beef Carcass Data Service to producers and beef industry groups, telling them how to subscribe and how the service can benefit them.

Former Information Division staffer **Jerry Mason** originally scripted the film, and he and **Bob Leverette** of the Livestock Division accompanied a camera crew to Omaha last year for initial filming. Steve and Bob returned with the camera crew to Omaha this year for additional footage. The Nebraska Beef Cattle Improvement Association—one of the Nebraska organizations serving as a BCDS cooperator by distributing official eartags to interested producers—helped with the filming.

About 75 copies of *The Connecting Link* will be distributed: one to each land grant college, and the balance to Livestock and Information Division field offices.

# Personnel Actions

## RETIREMENTS

### Dairy

**Helen C. Madden,** retired from the Boston Regional Milk Order, on March 31. Helen was an auditor with nearly 34 years of federal service.

**Elizabeth B. Pike,** also from the Boston Regional Milk Order, retired on March 31. Elizabeth was a clerk with 15 years of federal service.

### Grain

**Richard S. Cotter,** chief, Market News Branch, Independence, Mo., retired February 28 after 30 years of service. Dick transferred in 1967 from the Poultry Division's Market News Branch in Kansas City to head up the Grain Division's Market News Branch.

**Mildred DeFrance,** Peoria, Ill., Office, Inspection Branch, retired after 20 years of service.

### Livestock

**Emiel S. LaBorde,** meat grader at Dixon, Calif., retired on disability April 3. He began working as a meat grader at San Francisco, Calif., in 1943 and resigned in 1947. Emiel returned to duty there in 1951. He was transferred to Broderick, Calif., in 1962 and to Dixon in 1968.

### Poultry

**A. Elizabeth Handy,** home economist with the Division, retired April 16 on disability after more than 29 years of noteworthy service with USDA. She had been with the Division since 1960. Before that, she worked as a dietitian at Doctors Hospital in the District of Columbia and did research for USDA's school lunch program. Betty is a real "pro" in her fields of home economics and nutrition and has a wide circle of friends in these fields. She is respected and admired by all who have worked with her and will be very greatly missed.

**Henry F. Szetela,** agricultural commodity grader, Newark, N.J., retired March 15 after 30 years of government service, 26 of them with the Poultry Division.

## WELCOME

### Dairy

The following employees joined the offices of the milk market administrators in March:

**Peggy A. Banks,** card punch operator, Oklahoma Metropolitan Milk Order.

**Judith G. Brunner,** administrative assistant, Greater Kansas City Milk Order.

**Michael J. McDonald,** auditor trainee, Chicago Regional Milk Order.

**Deborah A. Moistner,** laboratory aide, Indiana Milk Order.

**Gardner A. Orstead,** auditor trainee, Chicago Regional Milk Order.

**Dale E. Shallenberg,** computer specialist, Chicago Regional Milk Order.

### Fruit & Vegetable

**Barbara Armstrong,** clerk-typist, joined the New York field office of the Regulatory Branch on March 3.

**Victor Harris,** clerk-typist, joined the Regulatory Branch in Washington on March 10.

**Carolyn F. Klotz,** joined the Specialty Crops Branch on March 2 as a clerk-stenographer in the Marketing Agreement Section.

### Grain

**Robert Kausch** has joined the Denver, Colo., office of the Inspection Branch as a clerk-typist.

▲

**Bob Laubis** is welcomed back to the Grain Division, as chief of the Program Analysis Group. Bob left the Division in 1967 to join AID in the State Department as a senior economist with the Rural Development Division, Latin American Bureau. A native of Kenton, Ohio, he served in the Air Force during World War II. Bob received his MS degree in agricultural education in 1956 and his PhD. in agricultural economics in 1959 from Ohio State University. Following graduation he went to work for USDA as an economist in the Livestock Marketing Division in the old AMS. He transferred later to the Grain Division.

### Livestock

**James Pendegraft,** who resigned to work for private industry January 3, resumed his position as a meat grader with the Division March 9 at Sioux Falls, S.D.

**Sharon Rimann,** clerk-typist, joined the consolidated office at Kansas City, Mo., March 23. She is replacing **Gailene Brown,** who resigned.

### Poultry

**Rachel Schwadron,** clerk-typist, joined the Philadelphia Regional Office, Grading Branch, March 2.

# Personnel Actions

## RESIGNED

### Cotton

**William M. Callicott,** supervisory agricultural commodity grader, El Paso, Tex., Classing office, has moved to Atlanta, Ga.

### Grain

**H. Hackett Cook,** agricultural commodity grader, New Orleans, La., office of Inspection Branch.

**Ernestine Hunley,** clerk-typist, Kansas City, Mo., Inspection Branch.

### Livestock

**Ann Marie Hritzak,** a member of the November 1974 training class, resigned February 14. She was stationed at Chicago, Ill.

**Nicholas Padula,** meat grader stationed at Bell, Calif., resigned March 15 to work for private industry.

## TRANSITION

### Cotton

**Larry R. Creed,** agricultural commodity grader, from Montgomery, Ala., to Jackson, Miss.

**Ronald H. Read,** agricultural marketing specialist, from Columbia, S.C., to Birmingham, Ala.

**Gordon Schofield,** agricultural commodity grader, from Birmingham, Ala., to Montgomery, Ala.

### Dairy

**Harry G. Berg,** computer analyst, transferred from the St. Louis - Ozarks Milk Order to the Chicago Regional Milk Order on March 2.

### Fruit and Vegetable

**Aldo V. De Santis,** agricultural commodity grader, PPS&I Branch, Los Angeles, Calif, transferred to the Regulatory Branch as a marketing specialist in the Los Angeles office, March 16.

**Mary Jo Evans,** who joined the Specialty Crops Branch as a clerk-stenographer in the Marketing Agreement Section on August 26, 1974, was reassigned February 16, to APHIS, Hyattsville, Md.

**James R. Frazier,** agricultural commodity grader, PPS&I Branch, Laredo, Tex., transferred to the Regulatory Branch as a marketing specialist in the Fort Worth, Tex., office March 16.

**Myla M. Schoeneman** transferred from the Regulatory Branch to the Vegetable Branch as a clerk-typist on March 16.

### Grain

**Delbert Davis,** agricultural commodity grader, Board of Appeals & Review, Standardization Branch, Beltsville, Md., to Rice Inspection Section, Inspection Branch, Hyattsville, Md.

**Charles Hunley,** market news reporter, Independence, Mo., to Washington, D.C.

**John Marshall,** national coordinator, to assistant section head, Grain Inspection Section, Inspection Branch, Hyattsville, Md.

**Lloyd McLaughlin,** market news reporter, Independence, Mo., to Washington, D.C.

**Dorothea Musick,** market news reporter, Independence, Mo., to Washington, D.C.

**Donald Osterkamp,** supervisory agricultural commodity grader, Inspection Branch, Philadelphia, Pa., to Board of Appeals and Review, Standardization Branch, Beltsville, Md.

**James Quillen,** agricultural commodity grader, Inspection Branch, New Orleans, La., to Board of Appeals and Review, Standardization Branch, Beltsville, Md.

**Pat Reese,** clerk-stenographer, Market News Branch, Independence, Mo., to Washington, D.C.

**Clyde Steves,** agricultural commodity grader, Inspection Branch, detailed from New Orleans, La., to Hyattsvlle, Md.

**Ruth Winner,** clerk-stenographer, Standardization Branch, Hyattsville, Md., transferred to APHIS, Hyattsville, Md.

### Livestock

Market News:

**Ronald Cole** - So. St. Joseph, Mo., to Des Moines, Iowa.

**Clay Thompson** - Des Moines, Iowa, to Columbus, Ohio.

Meat Grading:

**Jerry Frasure** - Ft. Morgan, Colo., to Bell, Calif.

**Wilford Hiles** - Dennison, Iowa, to Plainview, Tex.

**Peter Hitch** - Great Falls, Mont., to Bell, Calif.

**Samuel Keyes** - Philadelphia, Pa., to Newark, N.J.

**Charles La Franchise** - Omaha, Neb., to San Francisco, Calif.

**Harry Meisner** - Mason City, Iowa, to Albert Lea, Minn.

**Clayton Root** - Ft. Morgan, Colo., to Bell, Calif.

**Victor Rowland** - Bell, Calif., to Omaha, Neb.

### Poultry

The following agricultural commodity graders have transferred:

**Raymond P. Bair** - Wabash to Seymour, Ind.

**William H. Bent** - Trenton, N.J., to Gainesville, Ga.

**Mary S. Campbell** - Birmingham to Warrior, Ala.

**Jerry W. Duty** - Collins to Canton, Miss.

**Phillip G. Fehler** - Ripon to Modesto, Calif.

**Luther T. Goldman** - Auburn to Ashland, Ala.

**John Jelgerhuis** - Toledo to Tenino, Wash.

**Imogene R. Laughlin** - Washington to Odon, Ind.

**Dale C. Ocken** - Mt. Vernon to Toledo, Wash.

**Margaret Padgett** - Waxahachie to Carthage, Tex.

**Robert M. Pamperin** - Modesto to Ripon, Calif.

**Annette G. Parker** - Canton to Sabastopol, Miss.

**Bobby C. Porter** - Forest to Water Valley, Miss.

**Elliott W. Schroeder** - Sumner to Calmar, Iowa.

**Bessie L. Sweeting** - Ashland to Tuscaloosa, Ala.

**Videlia Thompson** - Carthage to Mt. Pleasant, Tex.

11

# Personnel Actions

## Information

Nancy Bevis, secretary to the director, joined the Division on April 14. She had been with Administrative Services since 1971.

## PROMOTIONS

### Grain

Conrad Herndon, supervisory agricultural commodity grader, Inspection Branch, New Orleans, La., to chairman, Board of Appeals and Review, Standardization Branch, Beltsville, Md.

### Livestock

David Pottorff, formerly meat grader at Plainview, Tex., was promoted to supervisory meat grader at Bell, Calif., March 30.

Tom Jennings was promoted from personnel clerk to administrative assistant in the Administrative Group, March 30.

### Poultry

Mary Ann Clark, secretary-stenographer, was promoted to program assistant, Market News Branch, Wash.,D.C., March 30.

David W. Jacobs, agricultural commodity grader, Lincoln, Neb., was promoted and reassigned to Topeka, Kan., March 2.

Josetta Lamorella, secretary-stenographer, was promoted to program assistant, Grading Branch, Wash., D.C., March 2.

### Information

Connie Crunkleton has been named regional director of the Division's Atlanta Office. Connie had been assistant to Stan Prochaska who was appointed director of the Division in February.

Before joining USDA, Connie worked for Atlanta Boatworks, Libby-McNeil-Libby Foods, and the Osborne Travel Agency. She began with the Atlanta Information Office as a clerk-stenographer in 1961. After working a few years she returned to school full-time (while working full-time), received a BA in Journalism from Georgia State University, and became a public information specialist.

Connie and her husband live on a small farm on the outskirts of Atlanta where they raise and show Arabian horses.

## AWARDS

### Dairy

Valarie Champlain of the Administrative Office took top honors recently in the Northern Virginia competition for Miss Future Business Leaders of America. Valarie, who is working under a vocational training—governmental program, is a student at Annandale High School. She has been with the Dairy Division since November 1974 and plans to remain in a part-time capacity as clerk-typist while continuing her education at Northern Virginia Community College in the fall.

### Livestock

Vivian M. Hamlin, secretary in the Market News Office at Phoenix, Ariz., was recognized in March for exceptional performance. She received a Certificate of Merit and quality increase for *outstanding initiative, efficiency, and administrative/technical expertise—contributing significantly to the effective operation of the Market News Office at Phoenix.*

John Mosbach, formerly a meat grader stationed at Ada, Okla., and since February 16 an employee of the Packers and Stockyards Administration, was given a Special Achievement Award *in recognition of outstanding service to the public by preparing and presenting frequent educational lecture-demonstrations on USDA meat grades and meat cuts.* John was very active in explaining the USDA meat grading service to consumer and student groups and 4-H Clubs in Oklahoma.

### Technical Services

The Automated Data Systems Group received a Group Special Achievement Award which was presented on April 3. The employees honored were: Delores Gresham, Sandy Elston, Joseph Hindle, Barry Van Scoyoc, Bill Parsons, Jim Stallings, Gene Skinner, Pam LaBossiere, Frank Tirado, Lue Hall, Nancy Hill, Al Impellitteri, Frank Boyle, Jim Buchanan, Jr., Don Whitcomb, Jr., George Palmos III, Hattie Britt and Jeanette Lewis. The award read: *for outstanding excellence in the performance of their duties and overcoming unusual difficulties during the transfer of Agricultural Marketing Service's Automated Data Systems Support to the Washington Computer Center contributing greatly to the effectiveness of the Technical Services Division's ability to serve the AMS programs.*

AMS Report is published monthly for the employees of the Agricultural Marketing Service of the U.S. Department of Agriculture.
Cheryl A. Palmer, Editor, Rm. 3080-S, Ext. 447-7608
Doris Anderson, Editorial Assistant

# AMS report

AGRICULTURAL
MARKETING
SERVICE

UNITED STATES
DEPARTMENT OF
AGRICULTURE

AN ADMINISTRATIVE LETTER FOR AMS EMPLOYEES

JULY/AUGUST 1975

## Personal from the Administrator

*Administrator Ervin Peterson wrote this column two days before retiring from AMS and setting out across country for home in Sacramento. Midst departing day good-byes to Secretary Butz and Washington associates, and closing the books on a career of public service, Mr. Peterson wanted very much to talk again personally with his people in AMS.*

I leave AMS (via retirement) with mixed feelings: with reluctance at separation from a fine organization and so many able, professionally competent, friendly people; but with anticipation of change, of reacquaintance with the great outdoors of the Pacific coast from which I've been too long away.

If in the time I've spent with you as your Administrator I've helped you to feel a deep and quiet pride in your work and in the value of your activities to the public we serve, to feel greater assurance of your value as a person, and to believe with stronger conviction that our political and economic system provides man's fullest opportunity for the pursuit of happiness, then my time has been well spent.

For myself these past three years have been enjoyable ones. The privilege of working with you as AMS' Administrator was a most satisfying conclusion to a career in the public service—one that has included service in county, state and federal government. Now, as I take my leave, I hope that in some measure I have honored that service even as I have been honored by the privilege of being for so long a part of it.

I feel that I am possessed of a great multitude of blessings. The experience of having shared in the work of AMS has further multiplied them for me, as I trust it has similarly done for each of you. For AMS is a happy place, one that combines high performance with good fellowship. May it always be so.

*Editor's Note: Mr. Peterson would enjoy hearing from you. You can write to him—or, if you're out that way, stop by for a visit—at 1210 El Sur Way, Sacramento, Calif. 95825* ☐

## Robison Retires from Cotton After 38 Years

Photo by Lester Shepard

He's come 600 miles and 38 years away from the "garden spot of the universe," identified on the map as Williamson County in Franklin, Tenn. Administrations and policies have changed, position descriptions and job titles have come and gone, but the focus of his career, King Cotton, has remained as constant as southern hospitality and as sure a source of satisfaction as bourbon and branchwater on the rocks on a midsummer's afternoon in Tennessee.

Andrew (or Andy) Robison retired as Director of the Cotton Division on July 31.

Continued next page—

He joined USDA's Agricultural Adjustment Administration in the mid-1930's, leaving USDA only briefly to get an M.S. in Agricultural Economics at the University of Tennessee. He returned in 1938 as a junior cotton grade and staple estimator, cotton field representative in Memphis . . . and it was AMS from then on.

With the exception of a two-year stint in the Navy during World War II, Mr. Robison stayed in Memphis, where he became the assistant area manager, until 1954. Then he transferred to Washington, D.C., as chief of the Cotton Division's Marketing Programs Branch. Seven years later it was the deputy directorship, and in 1973 Mr. Robison was named director of the Division.

Mr. Robison is a soft-spoken man who finds it far more enjoyable to discuss his programs than himself.

"I'm proud of the work of this Division," he said about two weeks before he left. "I think it has a challenging position providing cotton classing and market news services for cotton producers under the Smith-Doxey Amendment."

Mr. Robison can remember the time, back around the implementation of the Amendment in 1938, when "cotton buyers were in every cross-roads town to purchase cotton from producers. Most of these people made a good living," he said, "buying a very limited amount of cotton from the growers.

"Classing and market news services," he went on, "which put the producer in an informed position to market his cotton, have eliminated the local cotton buyer function and have contributed an enormous economic advantage in the cost of marketing cotton." By reducing the cost of marketing, the ramifications of the Smith-Doxey Amendment have spread beyond those trading in cotton, and now result "in a net benefit to the consumer, often in an immeasurable amount," Mr. Robison said.

With his three sons away from home now—Andrew C, Jr., is curator of prints and graphic arts for the National Gallery of Art in Washington, D.C., William Robert is a lawyer in Boston, and John Wilson is with the Telephone Company in Richmond, Va.—Mr. Robison plans to enjoy a leisurely retirement with his wife Elfrieda.

And what exactly does that mean?

"Just as little as I can get by with." □

# A Preposition Is Something
# You Shouldn't End A Sentence with

*Instructor Eunice Smith and former Deputy Administrator Dick Bartlett inaugurate Center with ribbon-cutting.*

Photo by Lester Shepard

"The concept of learning is an individualized one, with the student progressing at his or her own pace or rate of speed."

On that premise the Personnel Division opened the doors of the new AMS Clerical-Secretarial Training Center to 43 student employees on July 28. The Center is a part of the Employee Development Branch.

With the initiative from former Deputy Administrator Dick Bartlett, the go-ahead from Personnel Director Irv Thomas, the encouragement of Deputy Director Larry Thackston, and the bureaucratic stumbling blocks moved aside by Branch Chief Charlie Wakefield, the Center's Instructor Eunice Smith began one year ago to transform the concept of an individual training center into a working and workable program.

The idea for the Training Center emerged from an Administrator's staff meeting back in February 1974 when Mr. Bartlett urged the Directors to make the most of in-house training for their clerical and secretarial staffs.

The Personnel Division saw this as a directive, and responded with a survey conducted among all AMS supervisors in the D.C. area. The results were

Continued next page—

enlightening: 108 supervisors saw immediate need for clerical training; only 26 did not. In the survey, the supervisors said the greatest need was for a review of English Grammar.

As a result, all employees who feel that they can benefit from refining their skills will now be able to take courses in: English grammar and usage, typing (all levels), shorthand (beginning), and shorthand review and speedbuilding.

"My personal goal for typists in AMS is to bring all of them up to the 55-words-per-minute level with five or less errors," Mrs. Smith said.

Although classes are currently open to clerical and secretarial employees, Mrs. Smith said one supervisor is now taking an English grammar correspondence course through the Center. Reading and spelling courses will be made available next year.

For Mrs. Smith the Center has become something of a mission. One week before it was to open, she sat alone in her classroom, Room 2304-E of the Auditors Building, surveying with satisfaction the fruits of the past year's efforts. In readiness for the first week's students were class schedules, results of pre-tests,

English grammars published by Harcourt, Brace, Jovanovich, and the typewriters and tape players, or hardware and software as Mrs. Smith refers to them, that she personally selected.

Mrs. Smith is assisted by Boone Ferrebee, a trainee instructor, but otherwise runs the Center and conducts its classes herself.

After 18 years of raising a family, she joined the Personnel Division as a secretary in the Employee Development Branch in 1970. When Branch Chief Charlie Wakefield became chairman of the Planning Program Committee for the Conference on Instructional Technology for Government Trainers in 1973, she became his assistant. Gradually she adopted employee development as her own field of interest. Mrs. Smith left the secretarial field, went back in grade for one year to train as an employee development specialist, became a specialist, and then instructor of the newly-created Training Center.

Mrs. Smith said that classes are now being formed on the basis of the Interest Forms circulated among supervisors. The forms should be returned to her in Room 2304-E of the Auditors Building, and she is available there to chat with anyone who would like to discuss his or her area of interest. □

---

# Division News

## FRUIT AND VEGETABLE

### ● Lettuce from Field to Table—by Kuryloski

Don Kuryloski, chief of the Vegetable Branch, wrote an article, "Marketing Lettuce in the United States," at the request of the Senate Committee on Agriculture and Forestry, for a publication the Committee put out on "Market Functions and Costs for Food between America's Fields and Tables."

The publication was used as a background handout at hearings in the midwest on the nation's food marketing system. The hearings were conducted by the Subcommittee on Agricultural Production, Marketing, and the Stabilization of Prices, under Senator Huddleston of Kentucky.

### ● Hearings Held on the Perishable Agricultural Commodities Act

On June 24 and 25, hearings were held on the PACA

by the Subcommittee on Department Operations, Investigations, and Oversight, of the Committee on Agriculture, House of Representatives. Director Floyd Hedlund, accompanied and assisted by George Goldsborough and John Gardner, represented USDA. Seven members of the industry presented statements on the administration of the PACA.

### ● Processed Products Standardization and Inspection Branch Meetings and Demonstrations

Jack Barham, Ripon, Wis., area officer-in-charge described Branch activities on April 21 to the Racine-Kenosha Women's Traffic Club. Jack made a similar presentation May 13 to the Ripon Kiwanis Club.

Ron Urton and Kathy Rudolf of the Fayetteville, Ark., area PPSI staff, demonstrated the grading of various products to the Durant, Okla., High School Future Homemakers of America on April 28.

Quality control personnel at Draper Foods, Inc., Slaughters Neck, Dela., met with Officer-in-Charge

# Division News

Henry Schneider and Inspector Joe Logan, Easton, Md., area office, April 30, to learn about processed fruit and vegetable inspection activities. During the session Henry and Joe demonstrated the inspection of canned asparagus.

Quinton E. Cummings, San Jose, Calif., sub-area supervisor, and Reinder J. Groen, inspector at San Jose, participated April 25 in the Yerba Buena High School Career Week. Quinton and Reinder gave the approximately 140 students and teachers attending a brief run-down of PPSI Branch activity and then took on a question and answer session. High school students are sharp, and Quinton and Reinder reported that the questions ran like this: "Are all canned and frozen foods inspected by USDA?" "If a label in the supermarket reads 'Grade A,' does this mean the product has been graded by the USDA?" "Are all food processing plants inspected by USDA?"

Vic Levene, officer-in-charge, Richmond, Va., demonstrated the grading of canned and frozen fruits and vegetables on May 6 to a group of Food Service personnel, including the staff of the Virginia Department of Purchase and Supply, state dietitians, and buyers and food managers of institutions throughout the state.

Harley Watts, Van Wert, Ohio, area officer-in-charge, met May 14 with procurement officials, the Director of Food Service and the University Dietitian at Kent State University at Kent, Ohio, to discuss grading and inspecting processed fruits and vegetables.

John Teas, Fayetteville, Ark., area officer-in-charge, and Inspector Ron Urton, took part in the Bureau of Indian Affairs Southwest Regional Conference held May 28 at the Southwest Oklahoma College in Durant. John discussed Branch activities and Ron demonstrated grading various products.

Jim Hensley, inspector-in-charge of the Chicago field office, finds that the film, *Behind the Grade Mark,* is coming in handy for his presentations to classes at the Donoghue Elementary School and to primary and junior high students at the Bryant School.

Ted Hollen, Fresno, Calif., area assistant officer-in-charge, and Yoshiki Kagawa, agricultural commodity grader, addressed a class of 30 students in the Fruit and Vegetable Standardization class at California State University at Fresno in late May. Ted explained the functions of the PPSI Branch and outlined the types of inspection services available. Yoshiki demonstrated the grading of canned freestone peaches and conducted a Q and A session.

Sheldon Promisel, Rochester, N.Y., area officer-in-charge, attended the 89th Annual Convention of the Associated New York State Food Processors, Inc., June 5. Sheldon met with numerous representatives from New York state fruit and vegetable processing plants and allied industries to discuss inspection activities for the coming season.

● **Edwards Goes Live on Florida Broadcast**

Doug Edwards, officer-in-charge, Hastings, Fla., is now broadcasting live five minutes of cabbage and potato market information each day during the noon farm hour on radio station WSUZ in Palatka, Fla. Previously the broadcast had been recorded.

● **Federal-State Agreement with Michigan Revised**

The cooperative agreement with the state of Michigan has been revised to provide expanded volume information on all major Michigan fruits and vegetables moving to market by truck. Mike Pflueger, officer-in-charge, Benton Harbor, will take charge of carrying out the new program, requested by Michigan growers and shippers.

● **Market News Office Visitors**

Tom Cooper, officer-in-charge, Nogales, Ariz., was visited by the International Trade Class from Arizona State University at Tempe, on May 2. Tom explained the functions and purposes of the Market News Branch. Tom was visited in early May by David Warren an agromarketing specialist with the A.I.D. program in Guatemala and Carlos Roberto Claverie, with the Central American Institute of Investigation and Industrail Technology in Guatemala. They were particularly interested in discussing the potential for importing specialty crops such as sugar peas.

The New York Hunts Point market continues to attract foreign visitors. On April 9 Pedro A. Nites, National Federation of Coffee Growers of Colombia, (Bogota, Colombia), Francisco Cadillos T, Quito, (Ecuador), and Jose Nelson Rios (Panama), accompanied by their interpreter Liliana Milani, visited the New York City market news office for a review of the market news program and to tour the Hunts Point Market with market news Officer-In-Charge Tom Hill.

On April 10, Jose R. Espaillot Gonzalez and Francisco Miguel Gonzalez from the Dominican Republic, along with Jose Compres, their interpreter,

# Division News

visited the New York office for assistance in making contacts with importers of fresh produce.

George Asling, South Carolina Department of Agriculture, visited **John O'Neil**, officer-in-charge, Boston, Mass., and Tom Hill, officer-in-charge, New York City, N.Y. Market News Offices to discuss the marketing of South Carolina vegetables in each city and to visit receivers on both markets.

Gonzalo Segura, San Jose, Costa Rica, and Francisco Luna and Rafael Cardona, Bogota, Colombia, came to Washington June 6 to talk fruit and vegetable marketing with **Clay Ritter**, chief of the Market News Branch. Clay outlined the functions and scope of the Fruit and Vegetable Market News Service for the visitors.

**Tom Hill** had a few California guests in mid-June. Joe Hunt, federal inspector-in-charge in the Salinas district, and Norman Brown, Orville Sommers, and Jan King, supervisors for fruit and vegetable quality control, California Department of Food and Agriculture, came to New York for information about the area covered and methods used in getting supply data for the New York City metropolis.

**John Kennedy**, St. Louis, Mo., took Carter Price of the University of Arkansas on a tour June 20 of the St. Louis produce market, so Price could discuss the marketing of Arkansas tomatoes with various receivers.

## ● Price, Wofford Brief State Ag Officials

At the request of Roy Romer, new Colorado commissioner of agriculture, Denver market reporters **Clark Price** and **Clyde Wofford** briefed Mr. Romer as well as Don Svedman, deputy commissioner, Erwyn Witte, chief of markets, and several members of the Colorado Budget Committee on the market news program in Colorado.

## ● Honey Line Buzzing

**G. F. Pittman**, head of the Market Reports Section, Market News Branch, reports that the Washington telephone recorder installed in early June for honey is buzzing with more than 100 calls received per week. The recording is updated weekly with the latest honey and beeswax market information from the major producing states. The recording also covers imported honey.

## GRAIN

### ● Field Activities

Field Office Supervisor **Jim Phelps**, Chief Inspector Floyd Doucet, and **Hesser Westbrook**, all from Beaumont, Tex., and Field Office Supervisor **Rodney Hoffpauir**, Lake Charles, met with Port of Lake Charles officials to review bulk grain handling facilities there. Mechanical samplers are being installed in these facilities and the group inspected the installations to make certain they were satisfactory. Mechanical samplers will be required in all export grain loading elevators in the near future.

### ● Visitors

**Stan Rollin**, commissioner, Plant Variety Protection Office, reported that Dr. J. Sneep of Wageningen, the Netherlands, visited his office on May 13. Dr. Sneep is the technical leader for the plant variety rights law in the Netherlands. Stan explained the U.S. procedures for granting U.S. certificates of protection.

**Harry Schmidt**, Inspection Branch, New Orleans, escorted Dr. Fritz Dietrich, German Ministry of Agriculture, on a tour of the grain elevators in the New Orleans area. Dr. Dietrich was generally interested in the loading of ships and export facilities.

### ● Visitors From Brazil

On May 4, Edmond Missiaen, assistant agricultural attache, visited **John Marshall**, Inspection Branch, Hyattsville, to learn more about U.S. grain standards and regulations and various factor interpretations used in grading.

On June 3 Joao Oliveira, economist in charge of research activities, and Benjamin Martinez, coordinator of vegetable oil policy, visited with **John Marshall** and **Chuck Hunley**, acting chief, Market News Branch, Washington, D.C. They were interested in learning the whole concept of grain inspection in the United States. Chuck explained the objective of the grain market news program, the kind of statistics reported, the source of information, and to whom the information is addressed.

### ● Meetings

**Kenneth Bourgeois**, head, Rice Inspection Section, and **Delbert Davis** attended a meeting of the Rice

5

# Division News

Grades Committee of the Rice Miller's Association (RMA) in Houston, Tex., on May 28. A new rice inspections certificate—which would replace the round lot, lot, commodity examination, and origin inspection certificates—was introduced to the committee. The single certificate concept was well received, and plans to implement it are underway.

Ken and Delbert reported that attendees discussed the proposal in the *Federal Register* for required information on certificates under the Agricultural Marketing Act and the new hourly rate fees which became effective Jan. 5. RMA advocates no change in present procedures. Although initially opposed to the new hourly rate fees before their adoption, RMA now favors them.

**Les Malone**, acting chief, Inspection Branch, attended the meeting of the National Federation of Grain Cooperatives in Atlanta, Ga., on May 21. Les discussed current standardization and inspection activities in the Division.

**Stan Rollin**, commissioner, Plant Variety Protection Office, attended the International Meeting of Plant Breeders in Rome, May 20 - 25; the Federation of International Seedsmen meeting in Poland, May 26 - June 2; and met with the executive committee of the International Seed Testing Association in As, Norway. Stan is president of the Association. This meeting was held to discuss plans for the 1977 meeting in Madrid, Spain, and to resolve problems that have arisen since the last meeting in Warsaw, Poland, in 1974.

● **Knister Named Chief, Market News Branch**

**Russell (Buck) Knister**, was named chief of the Grain Division's Market News Branch on June 5. Buck fills the position recently left vacant when **Richard S. Cotter** retired.

Buck was supervisory meat market reporter in charge of national reporting for the AMS Livestock Division for the past five years. Before that he held supervisory positions in the Livestock Division's Chicago, Ill., Springfield, Ill., and Phoenix, Ariz., Market News offices. In addition, he has served as a Livestock Division market reporter in St. Paul, Minn., and Muncie, Ind.

Buck worked for two years in South America for AID (Agency for International Development) developing a market news system for Brazil. He spent o ne year as manager of Interstate Producers Association. Buck is

an Arizona State University graduate with a BS in Agriculture. He and his wife Beverly, son Steven, and daughters, Mary Jo and Karen, live in Springfield, Va. Son Mark is married and lives in Phoenix, Ariz.

## LIVESTOCK

● **Meat Reporters Hold National Workshop**

The Market News Branch held a national meat reporters' workshop at Columbus, Ohio, May 9-10. Both Washington and field personnel attended the meeting, which included practical meat demonstrations: **Jim Stroud** and **Curtis Green** of the Standardization Branch discussed fabricated meat cuts, and **Jim Hodgson** from the Washington Meat Grading Branch reviewed U.S. carcass grades. One session was given over to a discussion of recent changes in meat marketing patterns, including the shift from carcass sales to boxed beef, lamb, and veal, and the growing sales of prefabricated beef cuts.

Participating in the conference were **Paul Fuller, Jim Ray**, and **Buck Knister** from the Washington office, and the following field employees: **W. Jack Obermeier** and **Weldon Hall** (both from Des Moines, Iowa); **Ken Sherman** (Philadelphia, Pa.); **John O'Neill** (Newark, N.J.); **Joe Bray** (San Antonio, Tex.); **Gordon Duty** (Amarillo, Tex.); **Larry Johnson** (San Francisco, Calif.); **Rick Keene** (Chicago, Ill.); **John McKenna** (Bell, Calif.); **Clarence Zugenbuehler** (Fort Worth, Tex.); **Cletus Schmerge** (Greeley, Colo.); and **Billy Lange**, Texas state reporter (Sealy, Tex.).

● **NLGMA Conference Held at Columbia, S.C.**

More than 60 National Livestock Grading and Marketing Association (NLGMA) members from 14 states participated in the Association's annual conference at Columbia, S.C., May 6-8. Most attendees were state department of agriculture and extension service reps working in livestock grading programs.

Workshop sessions were held at the conference to review the interpretation and application of USDA grade standards to assure a uniform grading pattern among state graders. Feeder cattle and pigs, slaughter cattle and hogs, and carcasses from the slaughter livestock, were officially graded during the workshop.

6

# Division News

Division people were there, too. Helping with the grade demonstrations were **Fred Williams** (Fred's also NLGMA executive secretary), **Charlie McIntyre**, and **Dan Stilwell** of the Standardization Branch; and **Bob Jorgensen** and **Bruce Harding** of the Market News Branch. Dr. Gary C. Smith of Texas A&M University was a speaker at the conference. Dr. Smith reviewed the factors involved in developing the beef grades over the years and their role in cattle and beef marketing.

● **Feeder Pig Grades Reviewed**

Fifteen state graders from Missouri and Illinois met with Division officials at Perryville, Mo., May 15, to review the application of USDA grade standards for feeder pigs. This meeting was part of a continuing effort to maintain uniform interpretation and application of U.S. grade standards by state graders who cover feeder pig sales for market news reports under Federal-State programs.

The review was conducted by **Bob Jorgensen**, market news western area supervisor; **Bruce Harding**, eastern area supervisor; and **Dan Stilwell** of the Standardization Branch. Helping out were **Phil McFall**, market news officer in charge at South St. Joseph, Mo.; and **Joe Cordell**, in charge at Springfield, Ill. Phil and Joe technically supervise graders in their respective states.

● **Market News Activity in Iowa**

**Daryl Vanderflugt**, livestock market reporter in charge at Des Moines, Iowa, and **Bob Jorgensen**, western area supervisor, conducted a workshop in Des Moines, May 20, for eight state reporters and Iowa Department of Agriculture officials. The workshop gave the Iowa people some practical work in the uniform application of livestock grades and a review of market reporting procedures and terminology. Iowa graders cover 16 auctions throughout the state each week, under Daryl's technical supervision.

A livestock futures grading workshop was held at Sioux City, Iowa, June 3-4, for reporters from 10 field offices. These offices are responsible for accepting livestock delivered to settle Chicago Mercantile Exchange futures contracts. On the agenda was a review of delivery procedures and grading futures livestock (slaughter cattle, feeder cattle, and slaughter hogs) to assure uniform application at all delivery points. Proposed changes in feeder cattle futures contract specs were also discussed.

They came from all over to Sioux City. From Washington—**Paul Fuller**, **Jim Ray**, and **Bruce Harding**. From the field—**Bob Jorgensen**, **Tom Ferrell** (Greeley, Colo.); **Joe Cordell** (Springfield, Ill.); **Don Perkins** (Indianapolis, Ind.); **Marshall Ivy** (Omaha, Neb.); **Sheldon "Bud" Reese**, **Jim McElhany**, and **Jack Colley** (Sioux City, Iowa); **Jerry McCarty** (Amarillo, Tex.); **Gary Mills** (Dodge City, Kan.); **Phil McFall** (South St. Joseph, Mo.); **Bill Marshall** (Kansas City, Mo.); and **Howard Dinges** (Oklahoma City, Okla.).

● **Green Conducts Meat Acceptance Sessions**

**Curtis Green**, Standardization Branch livestock and meat marketing specialist, conducted several meat acceptance training sessions in Bell and San Francisco, Calif., June 2-6. These workshops were refresher courses for graders on the technical and procedural aspects of meat acceptance work. Curtis also conducts extensive training sessions in acceptance work for each Division training class.

● **Green, Stilwell Demonstrate Grade Standards**

Standardization Branch specialists **Dan Stilwell** and **Curtis Green** explained U.S. grade standards for livestock industry groups during May. Dan discussed and demonstrated the standards for feeder pigs at the Southeastern Feeder Pig Show, Cookeville, Tenn., May 22. Curtis reviewed beef grades and the Beef Carcass Data Service at the California Livestock Symposium, Fresno, Calif., May 28-30.

● **June 1975 Training Class**

The 18 trainees in the Livestock Division's June 1975 training class reported to field locations June 30 for nine weeks of on-the-job experience. This first field assignment followed two weeks of orientation and intensive training in the interpretation and application of grade standards, held on the Ohio State University campus and at local meatpacking facilities in Columbus, June 16-27.

The trainees, their colleges, and first field locations are: **Daniel L. Bauder** (Cornell University), Newark, N.J.; **Richard M. Bloom** (U. of Missouri), Bell, Calif.; **Ty A. Brisgill** (Calif. State Polytechnic U. - Pomona), Denver, Colo.; **Eileen L. Broomell** (Washington State U.), Omaha, Neb.; **Nancy K. Cook** (Virginia Polytechnic Institute), Denver, Colo.; **Robert R. Durham** (U. of

Washington in early September, followed by another week at Columbus for training in meat acceptance procedures. Assignment to their official duty stations (second field locations) will be in mid-September.

### ● Attention: Livestock Cinema Fans

Livestock Division field employees planning to appear before industry groups to discuss meat grading services may want to add another item to their agenda: a showing of the nine-minute, 16mm color film, *The Connecting Link*. This film—which describes in detail the Division's Beef Carcass Data Service (BCDS), how it works and the benefits to users—is now available for loan from any of the 11 meat grading main station offices, as well as from most U.S. land-grant universities and AMS Information offices.

Current BCDS records show that approximately 110,000 official BCDS eartags have been distributed to 32 cooperating cattlemen's and agricultural groups. The cooperators in turn distribute the eartags to producers and feeders. Meat graders evaluate the carcasses of BCDS-eartagged cattle and record the quality grade and other value-determining characteristics. The data is then sent to the tag purchaser, who uses the information to improve breeding and feeding purposes. To date, carcass data has been collected on more than 22,000 cattle.

### ● Veal Grading Workshop Held

The Market News Branch held a grading workshop on veal calves in Lancaster, Pa., June 24-25, to review the interpretation and application of federal grades for vealers. Participating in the program were **Jim Anderson**, livestock market reporter at Lancaster; **John Van Dyke**, officer in charge at Lansing, Mich.,

attending the program.

## POULTRY

### ● Stringer Attends Seminar

Dennis Stringer, market news national poultry products supervisor, took part in the National Broiler Council Marketing Management Seminar in Point Clear, Ala., in May. Dennis discussed our activities in market news reporting and placed special emphasis on the reporting of broiler prices.

### ● Newborg Meets With Delmarva Broiler Industry

Deputy Director **Mike Newborg** represented the Division at the Delmarva broiler industry's fund-raising diner in May in Salisbury, Md. The dinner was held to raise money to promote Eastern Shore broilers.

### ● Division Personnel Attend Fact Finding Conference

Key Grading Branch personnel attended the Poultry and Egg Institute of America's 46th annual Fact Finding Conference in New Orleans, La. They also visited shell egg and poultry plants in the Division's continuing efforts to maintain comparability in applying grade standards. Attending were **Dave Long, Jim York, Bill Sutherlin, Don Taylor, Jim Skinner**, and **Bill Blackwell**.

### ● Van Houten Meets With California Industry

**Bob Van Houten**, market news national egg and egg products supervisor, met with about 40 members of the

8

# Division News

Southern California Egg Dealers Association during the week of May 14. They discussed proposed changes in the Los Angeles cartoned egg report.

## ● German Requirements For Imported Egg Products

West Germany has imposed additional inspection requirements on egg products it imports. This will have an impact on U.S. industry as well as the inspection program. Officials of the Poultry Division are working with the Foreign Agricultural Service, Animal and Plant Health Inspection Service, and the trade to comply with the new requirements which become effective this summer.

## ● Gulich and Greenfield Teach School

Standardization Chief **Dick Gulich** and National Shell Egg Supervisor **Ray Greenfield** were recently on the faculties of two egg grading schools. The Northeastern Poultry Producers Council held its 44th school at Airlie, Va., June 15-18. The 45 students attending were from the northeastern states, Maryland, Virginia, Indiana, and Minnesota. The Southeastern Poultry and Egg Association School was held June 24-27 in Atlanta, Ga. Over 50 students from shell egg plants, carton companies, and state regulatory agencies in the southeast attended.

## ● New Yorkers Demand "Shielded" Eggs

Personnel at an egg supplier commented that it was almost impossible to get an account in the New York City area unless the supplier provided "shielded" (officially grade identified) eggs.

## ● "Egg Marketing Facts"

*Egg Marketing Facts - First Half 1976* was issued in July. It was prepared by **Opie Hester,** assistant chief, and **Ron Roberson,** marketing specialist, Marketing Programs Branch, and other Division and Department economists.

Published twice yearly, *Egg Marketing Facts* helps producers match their production with prospective consumer demand. This means more reasonable returns to producers with eggs at fair prices to consumers. *Facts* analyzes pertinent factors, but

doesn't make specific production or marketing recommendations.

According to *Facts*, egg production costs will hinge largely on the outcome of this year's corn and soybean crops. However, other production costs, as well as those for processing and marketing, will be greater.

## ● "Broiler Marketing Facts"

*Broiler Marketing Facts - Fourth Quarter 1975* was issued in May.

Developed quarterly, *Broiler Marketing Facts* also helps producers more nearly match their production with prospective consumer demand.

According to *Broiler Facts* broiler production in the fourth quarter of 1975 at the same per capita level as in 1974—taking into account the prospective supply-demand conditions for competing meats and general economic activity during this time period—should result in an average price of about 41 cents per pound, about the same as a year earlier.

## TRANSPORTATION AND WAREHOUSE

## ● T&W, TSD, FSD Work Together on ADP Study

The Warehouse Service Branch requested the help of the Technical Services and the Financial Services Divisions in evaluating the automated records system of Lewiston Grain Growers, a large grain cooperative in the Northwest. The point of evaluating the records system of this Lewiston, Idaho, co-op, was to determine the extent that automated records and calculation could be accepted and used in warehouse examinations. The trend now is toward using automatic data processing systems at warehouses; the Warehouse Service Branch is looking into these systems to see if they will help reduce examination time.

**Lloyd Provost** and **John Galenski** of TSD and **Bob Peterson** of FSD worked on this with warehouse examiners **Al Empey** and **Dean Steele** of the Portland area and **Rolland Hendricks** of the Prairie Village National Warehouse Service Center at the Lewiston Grain Growers in mid-June. The AMS people studied Lewiston records and examination procedures in detail.

9

# Division News

## ADMINISTRATIVE SERVICES

### ● Marceron to Post in Administration Conference

**Ralph Marceron** has been elected vice-chairman of the Information and Records Administration Conference. The Conference is a forum for the exchange of ideas and experience in all areas of information management, and it promotes professionalism among paperwork managers. The National Archives supports and sponsors this government-wide activity.

# Personnel Actions

## RETIREMENTS

### Cotton

**Barney L. Henderson**, Birmingham, Ala. retired on Disability in April.

### Dairy

**John F. Buhrman**, chemist, Eastern Ohio-Western Pennsylvania Milk Order, retired June 13 with 20 years of federal service.

**W.A. Carlson**, Chicago Regional Milk Order, retired May 30. Carlson, an administrative officer, had nearly 35 years of service.

**Barbara L. Emerson**, secretary, Boston Regional Milk Order, retired May 30 with 16 years of service.

**Raymond S. Henneman**, auditor, South Michigan Milk Order, retired June 21. Ray had 15 years of service.

**Harold D. Klein**, supervisory autitor, Indiana Milk Order, retired June 5 with 14 years of federal service.

**Marie D. MacIntyre**, administrative officer, Boston Regional Milk Order, retired May 30 with 41 years of service.

**Harold D. Norlander**, accountant, Minneapolis-St. Paul Milk Order, retired June 6 with 30 years of service.

**Leonard R. Schiavone**, auditor, Boston Regional Milk Order, retired May 28. Leonard had 31 years of federal service.

### Fruit and Vegetable

**Charles Bartos**, officer-in-charge, Processed Products Standardization and Inspection Branch, (PPS&I) Denver, Colo., retired June 30. With 35 years of service in the Branch, Mr. Bartos was the senior inspector.

**Leroy Brown**, officer-in-charge, Fresh Products Standardization and Inspection Branch, (FPS&I) Memphis, Tenn., retired June 30 after 31 years of service.

**Donald S. Matheson**, chief FPS&I Branch, retired July 3 after 40 years of service. Don spent his entire career with the Branch and served as Branch Chief for the last 11 years.

**Alan Collier**, agricultural commodity grader, (ACG), PPS&I Branch, Fresno, Calif., retired June 21 after 33 years of service.

**Emile Danna**, ACG, Fayetteville, Ark., area, PPS&I Branch, retired June 18 after 30 years of service.

**Melvin J. Otteson**, raisin inspector and supervisor, PPS&I Branch, Fresno, Calif., area, retired June 30 after 20 years of service.

**George O. Siconolfi**, ACG, PPS&I Branch, Miami, Fla., sub-office, retired March 20 after 20 years service.

**William C. Walker**, ACG, PPS&I Branch, Richmond, Va. area office, retired May 21 after 30 years of service.

### Grain

**Harold Heins**, ACG, Minneapolis, Minn., retired June 30, after 30-1/2 years with the Division.

**Robert Jenson**, ACG, Duluth, Minn., retired July 4, after 27 years with the Division.

**Robert Spohn**, ACG, Kansas City, Mo., retired June 20, after 30 years with the Divison.

**Marvin Somerhalder**, ACG, New Orleans, La., after 30 years of service.

**Harold Westbrook**, ACG, Omaha, Neb., on April 26, after 32 years of federal service—29 years with the Division. Harold started his retirement with a trip to Alaska in June to visit his son.

### Livestock

**Michael Browne**, meat grader at Emporia, Kan., retired on disability June 17. Mike joined the Livestock Division at Kansas City, Mo., in 1962 and also worked at Omaha, Neb., and Wichita, Kan.

**John Fraley**, meat grader at Sioux Falls, S.D., retired on disability July 1. He started working for the Division in 1956 at Waterloo, Iowa, and subsequently worked at Ottumwa and Spencer, Iowa, before being transferred to Sioux Falls in 1973.

**John Holcombe**, meat grader at Dallas, Tex., retired on disability June 5. He entered on duty at Fort Worth in 1953 and remained in Texas for his career, working at Houston and Paris, and since 1955 at Dallas.

**Robert May**, meat grader at Minden, Neb., retired on July 5. He joined the Division at National Stockyards, Ill., in 1965, and was transferred to Minden in 1970.

### Poultry

**Robert A. Dorsett**, regional director, San Francisco, Calif., retired June 6 after nearly 33 years of federal service. Bob joined the Division Feb. 11, 1946.

10

# Personnel Actions

Paul C. Gauby, agricultural commodity grader, (ACG) Norfolk, Neb., retired May 7. Paul has been with the Division for more than 15 years.

Robert M. Green, ACG, Brownwood, Tex., who was with the Poultry Division for almost 16 years, retired May 30.

Earl W. Klein, ACG, Detroit Lakes, Minn., retired May 24. Earl has been with the Division for nearly 21 years.

Betty E. Posner, accounting clerk, Chicago, Ill., retired June 21 after more than 26 years of federal service.

Sigmund Selinger, ACG, Lakewood, N.J., retired June 3. He joined the Division August 5, 1969.

Lyle E. Tucker, ACG, Denver, Colo., retired June 7. He had more than 17 years of federal service and all were with the Division.

## Tobacco

### Taylor Retires After 48-1/2 Years

Photo by Lester Shepard

Homer Taylor, deputy director of the Tobacco Division, retired July 31 with more than 48 years of federal service, 34 of them with the Tobacco Division. Prior to that he worked for the Post Office Department.

Homer was first employed as a junior tobacco marketing aide in August 1941. He served from 1949-1952 as area supervisor for the Puerto Rico office. In 1959 he transferred to Washington, D.C. to become chief, Marketing Programs Branch; and he was named chief, Standards and Testing Branch, in 1963. He was appointed deputy director in January 1974.

Homer doesn't consider this a retirement from USDA. According to him, he will be taking an "extended vacation" with his wife Alpha, in Siloam, N.C.

## WELCOME

### Dairy

Lynette Burton, clerk, Chicago Regional Milk Order, June 22.

Jerry L. Cahill, marketing specialist, Minneapolis-St. Paul Milk Order, June 2.

Richard M. Koirtyohann, chemist (trainee) Greater Kansas City Milk Order, May 27.

Judy C. Louden, clerk-typist, South Texas Milk Order, June 16.

Brenda M. McDonald, clerk, Boston Regional Milk Order, May 19.

Thomas D. Silverberg, auditor, Minneapolis-St. Paul Milk Order, June 16.

Gary M. Underwood, milk sampler-tester, Boston Regional Milk Order, June 2.

Richard W. Vonderharr, Auditor, Minneapolis-St. Paul Milk Order, June 16.

Linda D. Ward, clerk, Oregon-Washington Milk Order, June 16.

Karl L. Weaver, auditor, St. Louis-Ozarks Milk Order, June 8.

### Fruit and Vegetable

The following employees joined the Regulatory Branch in Washington, D.C., in June:

Grace A. Arrington, clerk-stenographer.

Julie A. Gentzel, clerk-stenographer.

Sarah A. Johncox, file clerk.

Lisa M. Swinson, clerk-typist.

Sheila D. Way, clerk-stenographer.

### Grain

Carol Andreason, ACG, Inspection Branch, Indianapolis, Ind., June 22.

Eugene Bass, ACG, Inspection Branch, New Orleans, La., June 16.

Stanley Burton, collaborator, Market News Branch, Washington, D.C., May 25.

Walter Clust, ACG, Inspection Branch, New Orleans, La., June 9.

Laura Di Toto, secretary -steno, Commodity Inspection Section, Hyattsville, Md., May 25. Laura transferred from AMS, Federal State Marketing Improvement Program Division.

Ervin Dominick, ACG, Inspection Branch, New Orleans, La., June 16.

Tim Engbring, Inspection Branch, New Orleans, La., on July 6.

John Ganz, ACG, Inspection Branch, Wichita, Kan., June 2.

Pierce Humble, ACG, Inspection Branch, New Orleans, La., on June 11.

Margaret Kinney, clerk-typist, Administrative Office, Washington, D.C., on June 16.

Russell Knister, formerly supervisory Meat Market reporter, Livestock Division, to chief, Market News Branch, Washington, D.C., June 8.

Miller MacDonald, plant physiologist, Seed Branch, Beltsville, Md., June 16.

Laura MacKenzie, clerk-typist, Administrative Office, Hyattsville, Md., June 8.

Samuel Masters, agricultural commodity aide, Inspection Branch, Stuttgart, Ariz., July 6.

Maria Miller, clerk-steno, Seed Branch, Hyattsville Md., June 1.

Donna Mitchell, biological aide, Seed Branch, North Brunswick, N.J., June 16.

William Nichols, agricultural commodity aide, Inspection Branch, Stuttgart, Ariz., July 6.

Bill Overbeck, grain marketing specialist, Standardization Branch, Hyattsville, Md., May 20, is welcomed back after an absence of eight years.

Larry Poindexter, ACG, Inspection Branch, Stuttgart, Ariz, on June 9.

Betty Strassburg, clerk typist, Inspection Branch, Duluth, Minn., June 2.

Karen Watson, physical science technician, from U.S. Geological Survey to Standardization Branch, Beltsville, Md., June 22.

Cheryl Willis, clerk-steno, Inspection Branch, Hyattsville, Md., May 11.

### Livestock

Donna Lamar, clerk-typist, joined the Market News Branch at Washington, June 23.

### Poultry

Elizabeth S. Crosby, home economist, Standardization Branch, Washington, D.C., June 22.

Lorri Dolan, clerk typist, Newark, N.J., Market News, June 2.

George M. Domanski, summer aide, Newark, N.J., Market News, June 2.

Betty J. Knuth, ACG, Madrid, Iowa, June 16.

Roosevelt R. Reed, summer aide, Grading, Chicago, Ill., June 22

## RESIGNED

### Fruit and Vegetable

Raymond Flagg, ACG, PPS&I Branch, Yakima, Wash., area office, resigned June 21

Charles Newton, ACG, PPS&I Branch, Salem, Ore., area office, resigned April 1975

### Livestock

Faye Adams, clerk-typist for the Market News Branch at Dodge City, Kan., resigned June 5

### Poultry

#### Grading Branch

Douglas R. McCay, ACG, Ames, Iowa, resigned May 27

Mary E. Marksman, student aide, San Francisco Regional Office, May 16

Rachel Schwadron, clerk typist, Philadelphia Regional Office, May 30.

Virginia B. Wolfe, clerk typist, Los Angeles, Calif., transferred to FNS, June 14.

## TRANSITION

### Dairy

Howard D. Leathers, marketing specialist trainee, from the Greater Kansas City Milk Order, to the Minneapolis-St Paul Milk Order on June 1.

Edward W. McEleney chemist, from the Boston Regional Milk Order, to Ohio Valley Milk Order, April 27  Ed also received a promotion to chemist at this time.

Normand J. Pruneau, auditor, from the Connecticut Milk Order, to the Boston Regional Milk Order, June 21.

### Fruit and Vegetable

John L. Coulon, inspector, FPS&I Branch, Newark, N.J., to officer-in-charge, San Juan, P.R.

Herbert A. Hooper, ACG, PPS&I Branch, Winter Haven, Fla., area office, to Denver, Colo. as officer-in-charge.

Larry E. Johnson, inspector, FPS&I Branch, Detroit, Mich., to officer-in-charge, Memphis, Tenn.

Leonard E. Mixon, officer-in-charge, FPS&I Branch, Cleveland, Ohio, to officer-in-charge, New Orleans, La.

Shirley A. Moyer, clerk-typist, PPS&I Branch, Baltimore, Md., since January 1960, to the Baltimore Fruit and Vegetable Market News Branch office as a marketing reporting assistant June 7.

Darrell G. McNeal, officer-in-charge, FPS&I Branch, San Juan, P.R., to officer-in-charge, Cleveland, Ohio.

Kathy Olson, clerk-typist, Washington, D.C., PPS&I Branch, to the western regional office, San Francisco, Calif., June 22.

Joan Phillips, clerk-typist, PPS&I Branch, eastern regional office in April 1967, to Administrative Services, Property and Procurement Branch in Washington, D.C., May 26.

Sam Saadati, ACG, PPS&I, Los Angeles, Calif., to the National Oceanic and Atmospheric Administration Service.

### Grain

Brenda Askew, secretary, Commodity Inspection Section to Office of the Chief, Inspection Branch, Hyattsville, Md., May 25.

# Personnel Actions

Lawrence Hains, ACG, Inspection Branch, Houston, Tex., to Inspection Branch, Crowley, La., June 15.

Doyle Hurley, ACG, from Inspection Branch, Houston, Tex., to Standardization Branch, Beltsville, Md.

Robert Jobb, ACG, from Inspection Branch, Seattle, Wash., to Sacramento, Calif.

Ken Swanson, head, Inspection Branch, to Standards Section, Standardization Branch, Hyattsville, Md.

## Livestock

### Meat Grading Branch

David Bowen — Cleveland Ohio, to Detroit, Mich.
David DeJoia — Omaha, Neb., to Rockport, Mo.
William Dykes — Gazelle, to Bell, Calif.
Lorenza Gooch, Jr. — Omaha, Neb., to Dallas, Tex.
Timothy Reaman — Sioux City, to Denison, Iowa.
John Rus — Rockport, Mo., to Hospers, Iowa.

Leon Kothman, meat grader at Friona, Tex., and a member of the June 1971 training class, joined the Washington Meat Grading staff July 14.

## Poultry

### Grading Branch - agricultural commodity graders:

Donald G. Alexander — El Cajon to San Marcos, Calif.
Lester W. Almond — Springdale to Rogers, Ark.
Randall J. Dammann — Los Angeles Calif. to Marysville, Wash.
Hearld L. Davis — Noel to California, Mo.
Fred Donahou — Oakdale to Turlock, Calif.
Larry A. Inman — Detroit Lakes to Theif River Falls, Minn.
Lorin Jones — Independence, Kan., to Noel, Mo.
Franklin A. McKeown — Sebastopol to McComb, Miss.
Richard O. Miles — Cucamonga to Yucaipa, Calif.
Frankie O. Nixon — Springfield to St. Louis, Mo.
Mary C. Seville — Apple Valley to Norco, Calif.
William G. Snider — Norco to Gilroy, Calif.
William G. Snyder — San Marcos to Norco, Calif.
David S. Steely — Farmingdale to Lakewood, N.J.
Virginia L. Thrash — McComb to Sebastopol, Miss.

## DETAILED

### Grain

Albert Hanks, Inspection Branch, Crowley, La., detailed to Board of Appeals & Review, Beltsville, Md.

Ray Levine, Inspection Branch, Houston, Tex., detailed to Inspection Branch, Rice Inspection Section, Hyattsville, Md., to write chapters for rice inspection manual.

Rosemary Pollingue, Inspection Branch, Houston, detailed to Inspection Branch, Rice Inspection Section, Hyattsville, Md., to write chapters for rice inspection manual.

Larry Troutman, Inspection Branch, Baltimore, Md., detailed to Board of Appeals & Review, Beltsville, Md.

## PROMOTIONS

### Cotton

Marie Chancellor, El Paso, Tex., has been promoted from administrative assistant to administrative officer for the Western Region.

### Dairy

Edward A. Bugbee was named market administrator of the Puget Sound Federal Milk Order on May 30. Ed, who has been with the Dairy Division for over 36 years, began his career as an auditor in the office of the Market Administrator in Worcester, Mass. In August 1951, he transferred to the Puget Sound Milk Order and was designated acting market administrator for that order in December 1954. Ed replaced Nicholas L. Keyock who died May 21.

### Fruit and Vegetable

Eugene Carlucci, regional director of the northeastern office for the Regulatory Branch, was appointed assistant chief of the Branch on May 25. He fills the position vacated by John J. Gardner, now chief of the Branch.

A native of Brooklyn, N.Y., Gene attended Cornell University. He was employed for five years with the Railroad Perishable Inspection Agency and two years with a private inspection service in New York City.

In 1950 Gene accepted an appointment as a fruit and vegetable inspector with USDA. In 1955 he joined the Regulatory Branch as a marketing specialist, a position he held until 1970, when he was appointed officer-in-charge of the New York office.

### Grain

Homer Dunn, ACG, Inspection Branch, Kansas City, to supervisory ACG, St. Louis, Mo.

Fred Kelley, Jr., ACG, Inspection Branch, Toledo, Ohio, to assistant field office supervisor, Norfolk, Va.

Harry Schmidt, ACG, Inspection Branch, New Orleans, La., to supervisory ACG, Kansas City, Mo., on June 22.

Wayne Schoneman, ACG, Inspection Branch, Indianapolis, Ind., to assistant field office supervisor, Minneapolis, Minn., May 25.

Harold Skinner, Standardization Branch, to national coordinator, Inspection Branch, Hyattsville, Md., May 11.

Robert Starling, to supervisory ACG, New Orleans, La., April 27.

Helen Steede, secretary-steno, Inspection Branch, Hyattsville, Md., to Director's Office.

### Poultry

Jack H. Brownlow was promoted to regional director, San Francisco, Calif., June 22.

# Personnel Actions

## AWARDS

Photo by Lester Shepard

Length of Service Award recipients (story below) are from left: Administrator Ervin Peterson; Connor Kennett; Associate Administrator John Blum; John Pierce; and John Reeves.

### Office of the Administrator

Administrator Ervin Peterson, now retired, took time out during his last day on the job to present Length of Service Awards to some of his top staff. Associate Administrator John Blum received an award for 35 years of service; Director of the Livestock Division John Pierce for 30 years; Director of the Poultry Division Connor Kennett, 20 years; and Director of the Financial Services Division John Reeves, 20 years. Mr. Peterson received a Length of Service Award himself for an accumulated 10 years with the federal government—with USDA from 1954-1960 as assistant secretary for federal-state programs; with the State Department's Agency for International Development from 1970-1972; and as administrator of AMS from 1972 until his retirement June 30.

### Cotton

Clifford R. Wharton, supervisory commodity grader, Lubbock, Tex., received a special achievement award in June for continuous outstanding performance and operating the Levelland, Tex., cotton classing office which contributed greatly to the success of the Western Region.

Jerethea L. Light, agricultural commodity aide, received a special achievement award in June for superior performance of duties directly contributing to the efficiency of the Lamesa, Tex., classing office.

### Fruit and Vegetable

Charles F. Zambito, acting assistant regional director of the Fruit and Vegetable Division's Regulatory Branch, New York, N.Y., received a Certificate of Merit for outstanding and efficient service to the Department, and to the fruit and vegetable industry in the administration of the Perishable Agricultural Commodities Act.

The award was presented to Charlie by Eugene M. Carlucci, assistant branch chief, and Harry Apostoleris, acting northeast regional director, at the New York office on May 30.

Charlie has been with USDA for five years and is originally from Elba, N.Y. A graduate of Cornell University, he has an extensive background in produce, his parents having been produce shippers and he worked for a number of years in produce before joining USDA.

Charlie now resides with his wife and three young children in Glen Ridge, N.J.

# Personnel Actions

*Harry Apostoleris (left) presents
Charles Zambito with Certificate
of Merit.*

James Ewing received an additional $250 from Incentive Awards Officer, Neil Porter, for his outstanding initiative and concern for economy in the expenditure of Federal funds and for his exceptional effectiveness in bringing about changes in the Grain Division's Section 32 programs. **James Coddington** and **Thomas Lutz** received $350 and $300 respectively for the same award.

**Leroy Christeson**, national coordinator, received $100 from Deputy Director, Howard Woodworth, for his employee suggestion that aided in development of a form to correct previously submitted billing document stubs.

The Commodity Inspection Section's Testing Unit received a total of $733 for their high efficiency during the first half of FY '75. They are: **Sarah Marshall, Randy Alexander, Lucille Tucker, Marian Cauble, Wilbert Matthews, Elizabeth Day, William Levin,** and **Henry Ikeda.** Lucille Tucker also received $65 for her employee suggestion that improved the mailing procedure at the Testing Section in Beltsville.

**Ronald Roberson**, now a marketing specialist with the Poultry Division, received $100 from Deputy Director, Howard Woodworth, for his employee suggestion to improve grading procedures in rice.

**Les Malone**, assistant chief of the Inspection Branch, received $100 for his employee suggestion to use standard wording in many routine dockets. This eliminated mandatory clearance by AGC of these routine dockets.

## Grain

Three members of the Administrative Group in Hyattsville, Md.,—James Ewing, Joan Barsky, and Donald Jump—received $40 each from Deputy Director Howard Woodworth, for their suggestion for improving the mailing procedures in Headquarters.

## Livestock

Photo by Lester Shepard

*Charles Murphey is recipient of American Meat Science Association's highest honor, the Signal Service Award (story next page).*

# Personnel Actions

## Charlie Murphey Receives Signal Service Award

Charles E. Murphey, assistant chief of the Standardization Branch, received the American Meat Science Association's Signal Service Award during the Association's annual meeting at the University of Missouri on June 18. The highest personal recognition given by the Association, this award honors members for *"preeminence in the lasting contributions to the meat industry and service to the American Meat Science Association."*

In 1966 he was honored with a Departmental Superior Service Award for his contribution toward the development of the beef yield grade system.

## Poultry

### Art Martin Receives "Good Egg" Award

Federal-State Grading Supervisor **Arthur Martin** (left) receives a trophy in recognition of his outstanding contributions to the Maryland egg industry from Dr. Clyde S. Shaffner, poultry specialist, University of Maryland. The Maryland Egg Council "Good Egg" Service Award is presented annually for meritorious service to the Maryland egg industry.

Art, as he is known to friends and co-workers, retired June 30. At that time his career spanned 43 years of outstanding, dedicated service, making him the oldest (in terms of length of service, that is) active Federal-State egg and poultry grader in the U.S.

**Eugenia Seaman**, supervisory clerk-steno in Newark, N.J., was awarded a Quality Salary Increase May 25 for *continuing excellence in the performance of administrative and clerical duties and the mastering of a special electronic word processing and transmitting machine contributing to the increased efficiency and effectiveness of the Poultry Division in the Newark, N.J., and New York area.*

**Hazel M. Reich**, clerk-typist in Chicago, Ill., was awarded a Quality Salary Increase March 30 for *continuing excellence in the performance of clerical duties and the mastering of a special electronic word processing and transmitting machine contributing greatly to the increased effectiveness of the Poultry Division in the Chicago area.*

The following awards were made for outstanding service under the annual performance awards program:

**Market News Branch:** *for sustained superior performance in market news reporting contributing greatly to the orderly marketing of poultry and poultry products.*
**Ray H. Anstine**, dairy and poultry market reporter, Pittsburgh, Pa.
**Harper B. Clemons**, supervising dairy and poultry market reporter, Los Angeles, Calif.

**Grading Branch:** *for sustained superior performance in carrying out the responsibilities in the grading of poultry and poultry products.*

Supervisory agricultural commodity graders:
**Edward F. Hoerning**, Philadelphia, Pa.
**Gerald Y. Robertson**, Chicago, Ill.
**Lars J. Tjelta**, Des Moines, Iowa

Agricultural commodity graders:
**Lester W. Almond**, Empire, Ala.
**Lester J. Ames**, Spokane, Wash.
**Leslie W. Bell, Jr.**, Dardanelle, Ark.
**Frederick R. Bestwick**, Cranston, R.I.
**Helen J. Broadwater**, Germantown, Ill.
**Howard A. Cavanaugh**, Esterville, Iowa
**Thomas L. Cloud**, Waldron, Ark.
**Glen L. Curry**, Marshall, Minn.
**Brent W. Golding**, Monticello, N.Y.
**Russell W. Harbaugh**, Springdale, Ark.
**Alfred Kiel**, St. Charles, Minn.
**Margaret F. Kronebusch**, Altura, Minn.
**Ted R. McCandless**, Burbank, Calif.
**Raymond J. McMahon**, Sioux City, Iowa.
**Jack R. McNeley, Sr.**, Kansas City, Kan.
**Evelyn C. Morlan**, Hamilton, Mich.
**Elton J. Newell**, Boaz, Ala.
**Gary A. Oaks**, Westland, Mich.
**Robert D. Poggio**, Elizabeth, N.J.
**Thaddeus J. Price**, Arlington, Tex.
**Wayne W. Schafer**, Ripon, Calif.
**Elliott W. Schroeder**, Sumner, Iowa.
**Arthur J. Storbeck**, Preston, Conn.
**Claude E. Watson**, Chicago, Ill.

### Special Citation Presented

The Alabama Poultry and Egg Association presented **C.C. McClure** with a special citation *for outstanding service to the poultry industry.* McClure was the officer-in-charge of the Poultry Market News office in Birmingham, Ala., from 1958 until he retired last year. The award was presented at the Association's annual banquet May 30.

AMS Report is published monthly for the employees of the Agricultural Marketing Service of the U.S. Department of Agriculture.
Cheryl A. Palmer, Editor, Rm. 3080-S. Ext. 447-7608
Doris Anderson, Editorial Assistant

# AMS report

AGRICULTURAL
MARKETING
SERVICE

UNITED STATES
DEPARTMENT OF
AGRICULTURE

AN ADMINISTRATIVE LETTER FOR AMS EMPLOYEES

SEPTEMBER 1975

## Secretary Butz Swears in Wilkinson as Administrator

*The Wilkinson family enjoys a light moment with Secretary Butz before the swearing-in ceremony. From left, standing next to the Secretary: Mrs. Donald Wilkinson, Mr. Wilkinson, daughters Nancy and Karen.*

Accompanied by his wife Betty and daughters Nancy and Karen, Donald E. Wilkinson was sworn in as the administrator of the Agricultural Marketing Service by Secretary Earl Butz at 8:15 a.m. on Thursday, Sept. 4. Mr. Wilkinson, secretary of agriculture for the state of Wisconsin since 1969, succeeds Ervin L. Peterson, who retired June 30.

Also attending the ceremony were Assistant Secretary Richard Feltner and Deputy Assistant Secretary John Damgard; former AMS Associate Administrator John Blum, who retired July 31; Deputy Administrator for Program Operations Bill Walker; Acting Deputy Administrator for Management Irv Thomas; Division Directors or their representatives; and J. B. Grant of the National Association of State Departments of Agriculture.

Mr. Wilkinson, 53, comes to the agency after a summer of great transition in the Administrator's Office, and months of unsettlement for AMS following the uncovering of irregular grain inspection practices among private grain agencies.

The press has called him a "welcome asset" to the agency because of his federal-state experience, and Deputy Administrator Bill Walker, who himself joined AMS three months ago, said, "To me he stands out when you look at agricultural leadership." Mr. Walker first met Mr. Wilkinson at a milk conference of state departments of agriculture in 1971.

Mr. Wilkinson acknowledged that he has done considerable thinking about what has come to be known as the "grain situation," labeled by the press as his "top priority."

Continued next page—

**Administrator Donald E. Wilkinson**

Courtesy Wisconsin Department of Agriculture

Wilkinson—Cont'd.

'I am sorry," he said, "that the vast high-quality state and federal grain inspection staffs have perhaps had their reputations tinged slightly because of this activity in the private sector. I hope AMS' relationship with Congress can bring about a program that can fill today's needs. I have long been familiar with the use of federal-state cooperative inspection programs . . . this is what we've had in the Wisconsin Department of Agriculture to handle the vast amount of grain going through the twin port, Duluth-Superior. We effectively handle one of the larger grain export points in the country."

In short, Mr. Wilkinson said, he favors a strong federal-state-private system with the elimination of any potential conflict of interest opportunities.

Mr. Wilkinson sees no special headaches in the transition from the state to the federal level because his 27 years with the Wisconsin Department of Agriculture often involved him in AMS and other USDA programs.

"I have known Don Wilkinson for 20 years, first as an outstanding state marketing official, then as a leader among state secretaries of agriculture," said John Blum. "He is energetic, imaginative, and competent. He has worked with AMS in many cooperative

*Mrs. Wilkinson holds Bible as the Secretary swears in AMS' new Administrator.*

activities and is a professional in the marketing field. He can be expected to maintain the tradition of professional leadership which has characterized AMS over the years."

Mr. Blum, who officially retired from his associate administrator's post on July 31, is staying with the agency for transitional purposes through Sept. 30.

Since 1955, when Mr. Wilkinson became administrator of the Wisconsin Department of Agriculture's Marketing Division, he has worked with the fruit and vegetable inspection program, grain inspection, the matching funds program, federal marketing orders for vegetables and dairy products, and the Tobacco Division, among others.

"It has also been my privilege while marketing administrator of Wisconsin," he said, "to go through the chairs of NAMO (Mr. Wilkinson was president of the National Association of Marketing Officials in 1964) and several advisory committees, including the matching funds committee of AMS and the National Meat and Poultry Inspection advisory committee. Mr. Wilkinson served on the Meat and Poultry committee from 1969 through 1975.

"I can't think of a more appropriate individual to have been selected for the post of administrator," Mr. Walker said. "He's had a working relationship for many years with USDA, he's been involved in the marketing aspects of AMS . . . and has a "broad background of experience" through the "leadership positions he's held in NASDA and related NASDA agencies. He is highly regarded by the member states of NASDA."

Mr. Wilkinson worked on several marketing committees of the National Association of State Departments of Agriculture and was president of that organization in 1974.

His experience in these associations has given Mr. Wilkinson a sense of solid organization, and he is acutely aware of AMS' high-level vacancies of the past few months.

Continued next page—

"I can't think of any entity that can keep up its efficiency with gaps in structure," he said. "My hope is to fill leadership positions as rapidly as possible" so the agency "can proceed to get the job done.

"I have always attempted to develop the pride of management team participation in our Wisconsin staff, recognizing that no one person today, especially in agricultural marketing, will have all of the alternatives or the answers. I've long recognized the high caliber of people in AMS, and I feel privileged to become a part of the AMS team.

. "I truly believe," he continued, "that agricultural marketing has much to contribute to total well-being, to the American farmer and to the consumer. I'm looking forward to participating at both the national and international levels."

Mr. Walker, too, emphasized Mr. Wilkinson's possible role at foreign and domestic levels.

"With the continued and increasing importance of our commodity export opportunities, and the challenges facing the credibility of those opportunities," he said, 'Mr. Wilkinson possesses the sort of energy and initiative that can be a valuable asset to establishing a high rate of credibility with customers both foreign and domestic."

With the Wilkinson children busy with their own lives in the midwest, Mr. and Mrs. Wilkinson will be settling down alone in Annandale, Va. Son David has completed a Masters degree in Architecture, daughter Nancy is a senior studying Christian Education at Wheaton College in Illinois, and Karen is studying pre-law at Michigan State University. □

---

# Market News Association Honors Three
# From AMS; Langston Named President

AMS took three top honors at the 18th Annual Convention of the National Market News Association, July 14-17, in Atlanta, Ga., and an AMS man, B.C. Langston of Tobacco Market News, became the first federal employee to be named the Association's president.

Paul N. Fuller, chief of the Livestock Division's Market News Branch, was named Market News Man of the Year. This is the highest honor given by the 18-year-old Association, and Mr. Fuller was the second federal employee to receive it.

The Association also presented a new award, the Distinguished Service Award, to three individuals, two of them from AMS. Don Lockhart of the California Department of Agriculture Market News Program accepted the award for former Administrator Ervin L. Peterson, who retired in June and is living in Sacramento. Mr. Peterson will receive his award at a special luncheon in California.

Another recipient of the Distinguished Service Award was Dennis Stringer of the Poultry Division. Mr. Stringer is the national poultry products supervisor, headquartered in Atlanta. He joined AMS in 1955, after working with the Mississippi Agricultural Extension Service, and has been a NMNA member since 1957.

When he was presented with the framed certificate and bronze-inscribed mahogany plaque, Mr. Stringer said he felt "elated and quite reassured that my efforts of the past were worthwhile. It gives you a warm feeling to know that this is a response to your efforts . . . getting an award from the people you work with . . ."

B. C. Langston also felt honored that his peers should elect him to the presidency of their organization. Mr. Langston, a member of the NMNA since 1967, has been first vice-president for the past year. He joined the

Continued next page—

**Paul Fuller, Man of the Year**

3

federal service in August 1974 as a Tobacco Division supervisory market news reporter in Raleigh, N.C.. Even in his nine previous years with the North Carolina Department of Agriculture, he said, he was "always with market news . . ."

Mr. Langston said one of the chief goals of his presidency will be to attract new members to the NMNA from those states not currently represented. He explained that at its start in 1957 the NMNA was entitled the Eastern Market News Association. It has now grown to include 350 members from coast to coast.

"The Association has so much to offer reporters in non-member states," he said, "in terms of improvements in professionalism. It's to their advantage to join: They may be having problems they can't solve. In the Association they can pick up reporting techniques and advice . . . all market news is similar to some degree."

Paul Fuller remembers attending the Association's first meeting, also in Atlanta, back in 1957. Like Mr. Langston he sees the NMNA as a highly worthwhile organization and cites its unstated purpose as "promoting cooperation between the state and federal (levels) which is essential for the national program."

Mr. Fuller has been chief of the Livestock Market News Branch since 1972, and has been with AMS Market News for 19 years. Outside of his receiving the Market News Man of the Year Award, which he described as a combination clock-plaque, Mr. Fuller thought other meeting highlights were the panel discussions on market news dissemination and

*Dennis Stringer (left) receives Distinguished Service Award from B.C. Langston.*

industry views of market news. He said that Dr..Noah Langdale, president of Georgia State University, who threaded the jokes in his keynote address with straight lines about market news, was "absolutely outstanding as a speaker." Dr. Langdale's message to the assembly was: "You're serving the public, so be alert to their needs. Change . . . don't let yourself get into a rutl'□

*President*
*B.C. Langston*
*addresses*
*the assembly.*

# From Personnel

The Personnel Division reminds you that it's your responsibility to bring to the attention of your supervisor any continuing differences between your work assignments and your position description. Discrepancies can seriously minimize the accuracy of your description.

What goes into an official job description?

Three major factors—and these are pay-determining factors—are considered in placing a grade, series, and title on a position: the kind of work; the level of difficulty and responsibility; and the qualifications the position requires—not necessarily those you possess. When positions are grouped according to these factors, all positions within a group are given the same grade level, the same title, and the same range of pay.

Your supervisor is responsible for assigning your duties and responsibilities, and seeing that your position description is up-to-date. A classification specialist classifies these assigned duties by grade, series, and title according to the appropriate Civil Service Commission Classification Standard.

Work demands and responsibilities do change, so the Personnel Division says, "When in doubt, check it out!" □

## AgFCU Is For You, Too!

Word comes in to Washington from the field that USDA people who are members of the Agriculture Federal Credit Union are impressed with the services they receive. They like the fact that the AgFCU is a safe place to save money regularly and an inexpensive source of credit, and they are pleased with the ease of handling their accounts by payroll deduction.

But the AgFCU, according to General Manager Ben Hills, is concerned that many field employees are not aware that they, and members of their immediate families, are eligible for Credit Union membership. Any USDA employee, except those eligible for membership in another work-located credit union for USDA or federal employees, may join.

Field employees can request information describing membership advantages by writing: Agriculture Federal Credit Union, USDA, Room 1320-S, Washington, D.C. 20250. □

# Division News

## FRUIT AND VEGETABLE

### ● Processed Products Standardization and Inspection Branch Meetings, Demos

**Harley Watts**, Van Wert, Ohio, area officer-in-charge, discussed aspects of the Branch's services with the Quality Control staff of the LaChoy Food Products Company in Archbold, Ohio, on July 10. Harley showed the new film, *Behind the Grade Mark*, and reports that LaChoy has a new film itself, featuring a clip on USDA continuous inspection with a closeup of Inspector **Ken Franck** . . . . . **Harley** held extensive product grading demonstrations for Kroger Company supervisory and sales personnel at Cincinnati, Ohio, on June 25 and 26. Harley described USDA inspection and certification services that are available to Kroger and that the company might use to advantage. Afterward Kroger officials said they would like to hold similar sessions in other areas of the country . . . . . At about the same time **Jake Vollman**, western regional director, was busy participating in the California Olive Association Technical Conference. Jake, assisted by

**Ray Hartwig** and **Lee Virag**, area officers-in-charge in Stockton and Fresno, Calif., helped John Kimball of the National Canners Association to set up an olive display and were on a panel reviewing the cutting results (reviewing the quality of representative samples for the olive industry) . . . . . **Joe McAllister**, assistant officer-in-charge of the Winter Haven, Fla., area, attended a joint meeting of the Citrus Central Quality Assurance and Sanitation Committees during the week of July 7. Joe reports that *Behind the Grade Mark* was shown during the sessions and that participants were particularly interested in discussing the desirability of installing sanitizing systems on belts and conveyors in Citrus Central plants . . . . . That same week Joe met with Warren Savant of the Florida Canners Association, and Dr. John Attaway of the Florida Department of Citrus. The state people wanted to discuss matters relating to the Grapefruit Quality Improvement Committee, and asked Joe to work up ideas for a housewife flavor panel to evaluate canned grapefruit juice market samples. That plan was presented at the Citrus Commission meeting July 22 . . . . . The Southeastern Peanut Association's 57 Annual Convention at Miami Beach was **Mark Grant's** order of business June 16 and 17. Mark is area officer-in-charge, stationed at East Point, Ga. He reports that shellers

5

# Division News

expect another good season but are concerned about the sale of peanuts on the world market since other nations can now undersell the U.S.

● **Margarita Morella to Food Study Program in Iran**

Margarita Morella, physical science aide, PPSI Branch, has been selected by Washington University, St. Louis, Mo., to participate in a six-month biological and anthropological research food study program in Iran. Margarita is a graduate of Washington University and has worked as an intermittent employee in the Branch for the past three years.

● **75-76 Citrus Crop**

Joe McAllister reports that citrus trees are still in good condition despite some of the driest June and July weather in Florida history. The 12-year rain deficit is now 100 inches, and the state forecasts that, unless there's a hurricane this fall, Florida will face a severe water shortage.

● **News from Market News**

**Darrell Breed**, officer-in-charge of the Newburgh, N.Y., office, reports that the services offered by the office were publicized in the July 11 issue of the Orange County Cooperative Extension Service newsletter. The Market News Offices at Hunts Point, New York City, and Bridgeton, N.J., also got some mention in the newsletter, which gave the telephone numbers and types of reports issued by each of the offices . . . . . The Boston Market News Office got some publicity this summer when **Gerald Becker** came on board as the New York Information Office's summer intern. Gerald interviewed and photographed Boston market news personnel for a brochure, released in July, outlining the fruit and vegetable and ornamental crops market news services of the Boston office. Gerald calls his brochure *Market News Service for Fruits, Vegetables, and Ornamental Crops* . . . . . **Bruce Rockey**, market news reporter at Yuma, Ariz., reports that dissemination of the western Arizona cantaloup market is up. Radio station KZUL in Parker has just begun to carry the daily report. Bruce says the new program features shipping point prices, shipments, and other related marketing data . . . . . On July 21 **Darrell Breed** began reporting truck shipments of Hudson Valley sweet corn for the

first time. This means that the Newburgh Office now reports truck shipments data for all commodities—primarily apples, onions, lettuce, celery, and sweet corn—covered in the market news reports originating in Newburgh . . . . . There's a new report coming out of Mississippi this season, the watermelon truck shipment report by **Jim Finazzo**, market reporter at New Orleans, La. Previously only the market for pecans had been reported in Mississippi. Now, says Assistant Branch Chief **Dave Vaughn**, an agreement has been signed for a regular f.o.b. (market price) report on Mississippi watermelons for next season, likely to be issued from Thomasville.

● **Mexican Grape Production Increases**

**Tom Cooper**, reports that the bearing acreage of Mexican grapes has increased sharply, and additional increases are expected over the next couple of years. Production of Mexican grapes is centered in Hermosillo (175 miles south of Nogales). The most plentiful variety is Thompson Seedless, followed by Perlettes, Cardinals and Exotics.

● **Market News Visitors**

Bob Riemann of the Middletown *Times Herald Record* visited **Darrell Breed** at the Newburgh Office on July 9. Mr. Riemann is preparing for an article on Federal-State market news work in eastern New York . . . . . **Bob Criswell** of the Minneapolis Market News Office was host to Ray Allen, Department of Commerce investigator from Chicago, on July 1. Bob gave Mr. Allen a first-hand explanation of the market news work and a tour of the Minneapolis terminal market . . . . . On July 8 Carter Price, of the University of Arkansas, stopped in to the Dallas Market News Office for information on the marketing of Arkansas tomatoes . . . . . That was the same day that Officer-in-Charge of the New York City Market News Office **Tom Hill** explained methods of handling wrapped California lettuce on the New York market to his guest, Jim Klustermeyer from the University of California Vegetable Crops Department . . . . . A little later in the month, on July 18, Tom had a visitor from Paris. He was Jean-Claude Balcet, economist for the Society of Technical Aid and Cooperation of the University of Paris, France. The Society, Mr. Balcet explained, is experimenting with growing several hundred acres of cantaloups (Spanish type) and Juan Canary-type melons in the West Indies.

# Division News

## GRAIN

### ● On-the-Job Training

*Five new employees get a chance to meet and chat at the Division's orientation session. From left: Darwin Green (Agricultural Commodity Grader), Kansas City; Al Humble (ACG), New Orleans; Deputy Administrator Bill Walker; and Bob Fiduk and Carolyn Bevers, both ACG's in Ft. Worth.*

About 35 new employees attended sessions of a 40-hour orientation program in Langley Park, Md., July 28 through Aug. 1. Attendees included agricultural commodity graders from the Inspection Branch; plant physiologists from the Seed Branch; plant variety examiners of the Plant Variety Protection Office; and marketing specialists and physical science aides from the Standardization Branch. This program was the initial phase of a formal one-year, on-the-job training program developed for new agricultural commodity graders.

### ● Board of A&R Holds Wheat Seminar

Eight agricultural commodity graders (ACG's) reported to the Board of Appeals and Review for a three-day seminar (July 8-10) on dark, hard, and vitreous kernels in wheat. The ACG's were: **Ron Dunagan**, Wichita, Kan.; **Don Grove**, Omaha, Neb.; **Bill Dowd**, New Orleans, La.; **Bill Skillern**, Houston, Tex.; **Frank Nelson**, Ft. Worth, Tex.; **Jim Davidson**, Kansas City, Mo.; **Roy McGee**, Beaumont, Tex.; and **Bob Probst**, Mobile, Ala.

### ● European Grain Inspection Trip

The Standardization Branch's **Dick Gallup** and the Inspection Branch's **John Marshall**, both of Hyattsville; **Bob Starling**, New Orleans, La.; **Danny Murphy**, Toledo, Ohio; and Richard Miller, vice president of the Superintendence Co., visited Rotterdam, the Netherlands, and Venice, Italy, to study ship unloading

# Division News

facilities and procedures used in handling U.S. grain cargoes. During their visit, from June 20 to July 12, they also sampled grain arriving from the U.S. to determine its quality. Mr. Miller visited Superintendence Co. offices to study their sampling methods.

## ● Research Project Planned in Japan

**Scott Hartman**, Inspection Branch field office supervisor, Ft. Worth, Tex., visited several Japanese cities—Chiba, Nagoya, Yokohama, Shimizu, and Kobe—as well as Taipei and Kaohsiung, in Taiwan in late June through mid-July. Scott was in the Far East to lay the groundwork for a two-year project with ARS to sample U.S. soybeans being unloaded in Japan and Taiwan. En route home, Scott sampled rice in Guam. This rice had not reached Viet Nam before the war ended and was being fed to refugees on Guam.

## ● Rollin is Consultant to Brazil

At the request of the Brazilian Ministry of Agriculture, **Stan Rollin**, commissioner, Plant Variety Protection Office, visited Brazil to explain the U.S. Plant Variety Protection Act and to help the Brazilian government draft a similar Act for its own use. From July 27 to Aug. 9 Stan met with interested regulatory, research, and seed trade representatives in Brazilia, Campinas, Londrina, Porto Allegre, and Passo Funda. He said that while flying from Sao Paulo to the falls of Iguacu and on the return to Curitiba he observed coffee trees that were extensively frost-damaged. This destroyed coffee acreage will be replaced with wheat and soybeans.

## ● Hoffpauir on TV in Louisiana

**Rod Hoffpauir,** Inspection Branch field office supervisor, Lake Charles, La., made the local news Aug. 1 when Channel KPLC-TV filmed him on location at a Lake Charles port as he was reviewing rice inspection activities. Reporter Kelly Lane had interviewed Rod earlier by phone about rice inspection and voiced the interview over the film footage for broadcast.

## ● Research Project on Corn Shipments to Europe

The Inspection Branch and Dr. Lowell Hill, a University of Illinois extension economist, are working together on a research project to evaluate the condi-

tion and quality of U.S. corn as it arrives in European ports. A cooperating export elevator is loading a vessel at 12-foot intervals; this increases the accuracy of sampling, since the sampling probe is 12-feet long, and can take samples from the bottom of each pile of grain. (Sometimes grain is loaded in peaks that can reach 20 feet, for example, so eight feet of the load are left unsampled.)

Cooperating elevators in Europe will unload the corn. The Inspection Branch will obtain and analyze the samples, and compare the condition and quality of the corn as loaded in the U.S. with its condition and quality on arrival in Europe.

## ● Nafzinger Is Host to Foreign Visitors

**Larry Nafzinger,** assistant field office supervisor, Houston, spends a good deal of time describing the types of U.S. rice, its availability, and U.S. marketing procedures to foreign visitors. A group of Iranians, for example, visited the office in June, and Mr. T. Kamishigashi, Japanese consul, visited in August.

## ● Early Alert Program A Success

The early alert program is successful. This system was inaugurated last spring to alert the Inspection Branch to potentially damaging factors to crops being harvested. For example . . . **Jack Cheatham**, field office supervisor in Houston, alerted the Branch in

8

# Division News

June that sorghum harvest conditions in south Texas could result in sprout damage. The Standardization Branch prepared and distributed referee samples of sprout-damaged sorghum to all field offices involved. When the sprout-damaged sorghum became a reality . . . the offices were ready.

## ● Standardization Branch Briefs Visitors

Ed Liebe, assistant chief, met July 1 with an Indian Wheat Industry team, sponsored jointly by Western Wheat Associates and FAS. The Indian flour millers were interested in standardization work as it relates to the flour and baking industries. The team toured the Board of Appeals and Review at Beltsville . . . Later in July, on the 24th, members of the Colombian Wheat Mission, also under the auspices of Western Wheat Associates and FAS, were briefed by Gail Jackson, chief, on the Division's inspection system and use of contracts to obtain the desired qualities and protein in wheat . . . On July 22 Gail and John Marshall of the Inspection Branch, took seven members of the American Soybean Association and J. F. Lankford, FAS, on a tour of the Board of Appeals and Review. The tour was like a package deal: The soybean people also got a grading demonstration and joined in a discussion of soybean standards . . . During his visit June 30-July 3, Vern Duke, Canadian Grain Commission, reviewed in depth U.S. wheat standards as compared with the Canadian standards. He observed the operations of the Board of Appeals and Review and discussed grain grading, inspection, and supervision as it applies to the Board's new monitoring system, which is used to check the grading accuracy of licensees and inspection personnel . . . Frank Kutish, National Farmers Organization, dropped by the Branch June 27 to discuss the history of and changes in the U.S. grain standards.

## ● Meetings

Eldon Taylor of the Plant Variety Protection Office, attended the Malting Barley Improvement Association's field day at the North Dakota experiment station in early August. The Association presented an $85,000 check to North Dakota University for barley quality research. Eldon toured the barley field trials at W. Fargo, Carrington, Minto, Cando, Langdon, Grand Forks, Alvarado, and Crookston, N.D., and at Moorehead, Minn . . . Howard Woodworth, deputy director, attended the meeting of the National Association of Marketing Officials at Estes Park, Colo., in August. He reported there was unusual interest in possible changes in grain inspection arrangements. During the meeting the NAMO representatives passed a recommendation to the National Association of State Departments of Agriculture that supervision costs be financed from funds appropriated by Congress. AMS proposes that supervision costs come out of inspection fees.

# LIVESTOCK

## ● Labor-Management Meeting

Representatives from the Meat Grading Branch and the National Meat Graders' Council, AFGE (American Federation of Government Employees), met in Sioux City, Iowa, July 28-29, to discuss the interpretation and application of the basic agreement between the Meat Grading Branch and AFGE. This meeting, required by the agreement, gave labor and management an opportunity to exchange ideas and identify potential labor-management problems. Bob Leverette, who is an assistant chief of the Meat Grading Branch and was a management representative at the meeting, said that discussions focused largely on personnel matters. The union representatives were very interested in the Fair Labor Standards Act; position classifications; working conditions; grader transfers; testing meat grading equipment, the role of national supervisors; vehicle costs, and the status of the beef grade standards.

Representing the meat graders were officers of the National Meat Graders' Council: President John Novak (San Francisco, Calif.); Vice President Bill Mize (Sioux City, Iowa); and Secretary-Treasurer Don Jones (Chicago, Ill.). AMS management representatives were Dave Hallett, Meat Grading Branch chief; Earl Johnson and Bob Leverette, assistant chiefs; and Main Station Supervisors Martin Swingley (San Francisco) and Andrew Rot (Omaha, Neb.)

## ● Market News Dissemination Increases in Arkansas

The Livestock Market News Office at Little Rock, Ark., is now providing daily market information to the new Arkansas Radio Network, made up of 14 stations. On

# Division News

*Bob Leverette receives the Superior Service Award from Secretary Butz.*

July 1 the Network started programming agricultural news flashes throughout the day. The Little Rock Office, headed by **Bill Fulton**, provides a short summary of national markets each morning and a summary of the Arkansas hog markets in the afternoon.

The Little Rock Office is also now submitting livestock market news information for a new monthly newsletter produced by the Extension Service and distributed throughout Arkansas. This information includes quotations on livestock, plus monthly cattle, hogs, and feeder pig receipts.

#### ● Leverette Receives Superior Service Award

The Livestock Division caught up on some unfinished business Aug. 5 when it arranged for **Bob Leverette** to belatedly receive a Departmental Superior Service Award from **Secretary Earl Butz**.

Bob, assistant chief of the Meat Grading Branch, was unable to attend the public ceremony held in May.

Quite an AMS contingent came along to attend the ceremony in the Secretary's Office: Associate Administrator (ret.) **John Blum**; Deputy Administrator **Bill Walker**; Director of the Livestock Division **John Pierce**; and Meat Grading Branch Chief **Dave Hallett**.

Bob was honored for his work in developing the Beef Carcass Data Service, a joint USDA and cattle and beef industry effort to help cattle producers and feeders get information on the quality and yield grade characteristics of the carcasses their cattle produce. The BCDS began three years ago as a pilot project involving 10,000 head of eartagged cattle in four states, and has grown into a nationwide system returning data to producers on over 100,000 tagged animals across the country.

"I was very pleased to receive the award," Bob said. "I would like to comment that the success of this serv-

10

# Division News

ice to date is due largely to the efforts of field supervisors, graders, and clerks. The program keeps expanding, but no personnel have been added . . . I think this testifies to the fact that the people in the field are really trying to make it work."

## ● Texas Hog Grading Program Expands

The hog grading program in Texas, which started in Amarillo on a weekly basis in August 1974, has been expanded to three days a week at Amarillo and Lubbock. A second state grader trained recently and began grading in late June, and a third grader is now being trained. The hogs are graded by state employees according to USDA standards and then are sold in uniform grade lots. **Jerry McCarty**, officer-in-charge of the Amarillo Market News Office, is providing ongoing technical supervision to assure accurate application of USDA grade standards.

## ● Perkins Speaks Before Farm Broadcasters

**Don Perkins**, officer-in-charge of the Livestock Market News Office at Peoria, Ill., discussed USDA responsibilities in accepting livestock delivered to satisfy futures contracts for a group of prominent U.S. farm broadcasters at the Peoria stockyards on June 30. (Market news reporters regularly certify livestock for grade and weight specifications to meet the terms of futures commodity contracts.) About 100 broadcasters, all members of the National Association of Farm Broadcasters (NAFB), were attending the four-day NAFB annual convention at Chicago, and flew to the Peoria stockyards for the day.

## POULTRY

## ● Egg Film Plays During Consumer Carnival

*Egg Grades—A Matter of Quality* played continuously in the Department's Patio Theatre for Washington employees and visitors from the Mall during USDA's Consumer Carnival the week of Aug. 18. AMS employees, most of them from the Information Division, also staffed an exhibit during the Carnival and distributed the "How to Buy" publications.

## ● State Fair Time

Visitors to the Illinois State Fair in August received consumer materials about poultry and eggs and had a chance to discuss Division programs with **Dale Shearer**, Grading Branch regional director, Chicago, Ill.

## ● Market News on the Air

**Preston McDonald**, officer-in-charge of the Jackson, Miss., Office, began early evening live broadcasts on poultry market news on June 30, through the facilities of the Mississippi Radio News Network. The broadcasts, requested by the Network, are on a daily basis.

## ● Market News Offices Merge

To use manpower more effectively, the Birmingham, Ala., Poultry News Office was merged July 1 with the Atlanta, Ga., Office. On Sept. 15 Atlanta Reporters **Lyndon Wann** and **Jim Reed** will be joined by **Johnny Freeman** who is coming in from Des Moines.

## ● Wruk Meets With Egg Pricing Committee

Market News Branch Chief **Ray Wruk** participated in the July 24 meeting in New York City of the National Egg Pricing System Study Committee. The Committee, which meets periodically, continues to wrestle with problems of egg price discovery (the effort to find pricing systems for eggs).

## ● Grade A On Display

The Fernandes Supermarket chain, which has approximately 40 stores located in southern New England, recently added a two-foot square U.S. Grade A poultry shield to its window display. The firm's vice-president said even further promotion is planned using the shield.

11

# Division News

## TRANSPORTATION AND WARE-HOUSE

### ● Export Investigations: Bringing You Up to Date

Grain export elevators and independent inspection and weighing agencies in Gulf Ports have been under investigation for about two years by, among others, the FBI, USDA's Office of Investigation, and local law officials. They have also been under investigation by a federal grand jury.

To date there have been 63 indictments of 50 individuals, and three corporative indictments. The Division has suspended the licenses, issued under authority of the U.S. Warehouse Act, of 24 persons who grade or weigh grain, or both. Fourteen of the suspended inspectors also held licenses under the U.S. Grain Standards Act.

Among the indictment charges were: accepting bribes in connection with ship stowage; conspiring to steal grain in interstate commerce; falsifying certifications; defrauding the U.S.; violating the U.S. Warehouse Act; evading income taxes; defrauding by wire; interfering with USDA's lawful regulatory functions; obtaining money under false pretenses, and covering up material facts on the handling of grain.

### ● Kepley Assists Indianapolis Area

Homer Kepley, warehouse examiner in the Warehouse Service Branch's Atlanta, Ga., Area, helped the Indianapolis Area perform original, subsequent, and special examinations at processed commodity warehouses in the northeast last month. Homer's assignments, from Aug. 4-22, took him to New Haven and Hartford, Conn.; Boston, Springfield, Worchester, Lowell, and Lawrence, Mass.; and to Burlington and Essex Junction, Vt. The Indianapolis area staff says it appreciated Homer's help since retirements and illness had taken their toll on their personnel.

## INFORMATION

### ● Chicago Prepares for the Secretary

Secretary Butz kept the Chicago Office busy at the end of August, making media arrangements for his visits to Peoria for the Presidential Conference on Agriculture, to the National Livestock and Meat Board press conference in Chicago, and to the 2nd Ag Conference in Milwaukee. The Chicago Office reports that on Aug. 25, at the Milwaukee conference, the Secretary had media appearances scheduled from 8:30 a.m. until 3:30 p.m., with each radio, TV, and newspaper reporter getting a 15-minute interview during the day.

---

# Personnel Actions

## RETIREMENTS

### Cotton

Roanne B. Hamilton, statistical assistant, Market News Section, Memphis, Tenn., with 21 years of service.

Garland Perry, physical science aide, Clemson, S.C., after nearly 31 years of service.

Joseph T. Rouse, head, Testing Section, Memphis, Tenn., with nearly 39 years of service.

Jimmie Williams, physical science aide, Standards Preparation and Distribution Section, Memphis, Tenn., after nearly 22 years of service.

### Dairy

Edward A. Bugbee, market administrator for the Puget Sound Milk Order, retired on July 31 with 36 years of federal service.

# Personnel Actions

**Earl E. Gulland,** market administrator for the Duluth-Superior Milk Order, retired July 31 with nearly 32 years of service.

**Alfred Planting,** dairy products marketing specialist in the Order Formulation Staff, retired July 31 after 15 years of federal service.

**Fred L. Shipley,** market administrator for the St. Louis-Ozarks Milk Order, retired July 31 with 41 years of federal service.

**Elroy J. Stimpert,** from the Eastern Ohio-Western Pennsylvania Milk Order, retired July 5 with 32 years of service.

**Evelyn G. Zell,** a clerk in the St. Louis-Ozarks Milk Order, retired July 28 with nearly eight years of service.

## Fruit and Vegetable

**Minton C. Erickson,** western regional supervisor, Fresh Products Standardization and Inspection Branch, retired July 31 after 34 years of government service. Erickson has served as regional supervisor for the last 20 years. USDA will have his services as a re-employed annuitant for a short while.

## Grain

**Jean Frank,** reporter, Market News Branch, retired June 27 after 32 years of federal service.

**Howard Martin,** agricultural commodity grader, Inspection Branch, Omaha, Neb., retired July 31 after 27 years with the Division.

## Livestock

**John J. O'Neill,** officer-in-charge of the Market News Office at Newark, N.J., retired July 31, after 31 years of federal service. John joined the Division as a meat grader at New York City in 1951 and transferred to the Market News Branch as a meat market reporter in 1953. He remained in New York City until 1968, when the Division consolidated office was moved to Newark.

**Kenneth B. Sherman,** officer-in-charge of the Market News Office at Philadelphia, Pa., retired July 31, completing more than 32 years of federal service. Ken joined the Division at New York City in 1943 and was transferred to Philadelphia as a meat market reporter in 1950.

**Marvin J. Nordgren,** program assistant in charge of preparing the weekly Market News Summary in the Washington Market News Branch, retired July 31, after 32 years of federal service. Marv began working for the Market News Branch at Sioux City, Iowa, in 1952 and transferred to Washington in 1963.

**Robert J. Kaufmann,** meat grader at Denver, Colo., retired on disability July 31. Bob joined the Division at South St. Paul, Minn., in 1943 and also worked at Austin, Minn., before transferring to Denver in 1963.

**Magnus A. Modene,** meat grader at Austin, Minn., retired July 31. He began working for the Division at South St. Paul, Minn., in April 1952 and a month later transferred to Austin, where he worked for his entire career.

**Edward C. Hammie,** teletypist for the Market News Branch at Philadelphia, Pa., retired July 31, completing almost 34 years of federal service. He transferred from the Administrative Services Division to the Livestock Division office at Philadelphia in 1969.

## Poultry

### Agricultural Commodity Graders:

**Raymond P. Bair,** Seymour, Ind., retired July 28 after almost 20 years of government service. Ray had almost 18 years with the Division.

**Paul R. Blaskowsky,** Jasper, Tex., who began his government career with the Division in August 1958, retired July 31.

**Fred Donahou,** Turlock, Calif., retired July 31 after 20 years with the Division.

**Harold D. Faulk,** Jasper, Tex., retired July 1. He had been with the Division since October 1968.

**Raymond D. Wortman,** Jackson, Miss., retired July 31. Ray was with the Division for 21 years.

## WELCOME

### Cotton

**Carolyn J. Bennett,** chief clerk, Columbia, S.C.

### Dairy

**Nancy Clancy,** Washington, D.C., Order Formulation Staff, secretary-stenographer, June 22.

**Harriette Y. Freeman,** laboratory aide, Texas Milk Order, July 7.

**Eugene Kerstein,** agricultural commodity grader, Chicago, Ill., Regional Office, May 25.

**Pamela Klutts,** clerk-typist, Washington, D.C., Order Formulation Staff, June 8.

**William E. McDonald,** auditor (trainee), Chicago, Ill., Regional Milk Order, July 20.

**Mary Muster,** clerk-stenographer, Washington, D.C., Market Information Branch, June 22.

**Spencer H. Nease,** computer specialist, Minneapolis-St. Paul Milk Order, July 7.

**Donald O. Nelson,** marketing specialist, Minneapolis-St. Paul Milk Order, July 14.

**David L. Robinson,** auditor, Oregon-Washington Milk Order, July 6.

**Lee Ann Sweeney,** clerk-stenographer, Chicago, Ill., Regional Milk Order, July 6.

# Personnel Actions

Pamela Teaney, clerk-typist, Chicago, Ill., Laboratory, July 6.

Faye J. Tempin, computer programmer (trainee), Chicago, Ill., Regional Milk Order, July 6.

### Fruit and Vegetable

Milton Gray, agricultural commodity grader (ACG), Fresh Products Standardization and Inspection (FPS&I) Branch, Boston, Mass.

Larry Ivaska, ACG, FPS&I Branch, Pittsburgh, Pa.

We welcome the following clerk-stenographers to the Regulatory Branch in Washington, D.C.:

Beverly Chedester, Jackie Emmer, Grace Ferro and Natalie M. Pershatsch

### Grain

James J. Crean, ACG, Inspection Branch, Kansas City, Mo.

Barbara Diver, ACG, Inspection Branch, Minneapolis, Minn.

Larry Dosier, assistant plant variety examiner, Plant Variety Protection Office, Beltsville, Md.

Russell Frank, ACG, Inspection Branch, Indianapolis, Ind.

Thad Frey, plant variety examiner trainee, Plant Variety Protection Office, Beltsville, Md.

Dave Fulks, ACG, Inspection Branch, Houston, Tex.

Darwin Green, ACG, Inspection Branch, Kansas City, Mo.

Mary Haselow, ACG, Inspection Branch, Portland, Ore.

Bryan Hofer, ACG, Inspection Branch, Portland Ore.

Charles V. Marshall, ACG, Inspection Branch, Kansas City, Mo.

Terry Mason, ACG, Standardization Branch, Beltsville, Md.

Steve North, ACG, Inspection Branch, New Orleans, La.

Patricia O'Donnell, clerk-typist, Inspection Branch, Hyattsville, Md.

Richard Payne, plant physiologist, Seed Branch, Beltsville, Md.

Lawrence Poling, ACG, Inspection Branch, Houston, Tex.

Walter Rust, ACG, Inspection Branch, Stuttgart, Ark.

Hardip Singh, ACG, Inspection Branch, Wichita, Kan.

Gil Waibel, ACG, Standardization Branch, Beltsville, Md.

James A. Whisonant, ACG, Inspection Branch, Norfolk, Va.

### Livestock

James Clark, program assistant, joined the Market News Branch at Washington, D.C., Aug. 17. Jim previously worked for the Division (until May 1974) as supervisory clerk at the Kansas City, Mo., office.

Michael May, a livestock and meat marketing specialist, joined the Standardization Branch at Washington, D.C., Aug. 3.

### Poultry

Lucille S. Brown, assistant administrative officer, Grading Branch, Chicago, Ill., July 27.

Calvin S. Jones, Jr., ACG, Cortland, Ind., July 13.

Janice M. Sikora, clerk-steno, Grading Branch, Washington, D.C., July 7.

### Administrative Services

Tony Dimech, clerk, Supply Unit, Washington, D.C., July 20.

### Information

Barbara Kohn joined the midwest regional information office in Chicago in June. Barbara is a public information specialist.

## RESIGNED

### Cotton

Evelyn Henry, clerk-typist, Southern Region Office, Memphis, Tenn.

Ronnie Murphy, ACG, Hayti, Mo.

### Fruit and Vegetable

Brenda Getz, inspector in the Battle Creek, Mich., area, resigned July 5, to become a proprietor of a variety store in western Michigan.

Jerry Flowers, inspector, Dallas, Tex., resigned in June. Jerry is now a representative for Allied Supermarkets in Detroit, Mich.

### Grain

Berley Nall, agricultural commodity aide, Inspection Branch, Jonesboro, Ark.

### Poultry

James D. Hood, ACG, Union Springs, Ala., July 12.

Dayle Kurth, clerk-typist, Market News Branch, Chicago, Ill., July 4.

## TRANSITION

### Cotton

Helen Donnelly, administrative assistant, Washington, D.C. to Fruit and Vegetable Division.

### Livestock

### Meat Grading Branch

Larry Meadows - Pampa, Tex., to Friona, Tex.

# Personnel Actions

Merritt Pike - Amarillo, Tex., to Pampa, Tex.

James Rule - Mason City, Iowa, to Minong, Wis.

## Market News Branch

Lowell Serfling - Indianapolis, Ind., to N. Portland, Ore.

## Poultry

### Agricultural Commodity Graders:

Johnnie H. Adkins, Los Angeles to Santa Ana, Calif.

Joe M. Callihan, California to Sedalia, Mo.

Sharron K. Callihan, California to Sedalia, Mo.

Paul E. Coughlin, San Francisco to Oakland, Calif.

Luther B. Crownover, Laurel to Canton, Miss.

Blondena Dombroski, assistant administrative officer, Grading Branch, Chicago, Ill., to Office of Investigation, USDA, July 12.

Jerry W. Duty, Canton to Laurel, Miss.

Ellis R. Foster, Tupelo to Water Valley, Miss.

Curtis B. Germany, Union Springs to Guntersville, Ala.

Kenneth L. Lissman, Los Angeles to Santa Ana, Calif.

Marjorie K. Merryman, West Olive to Grand Rapids, Mich.

Jack W. Mires, Los Angeles to Santa Ana, Calif.

Debra Winkleman, clerk-steno, Grading Branch, Washington, D.C., to Financial Services Division, July 20.

## PROMOTIONS

### Cotton

William R. Crockett, ACG, Lubbock, Tex., to supervisory commodity grader.

Ronald Greene, Phoenix, Ariz., from marketing specialist to commodity grader.

Ronald Read, Birmingham, Ala., from marketing specialist to commodity grader.

### Fruit and Vegetable

#### Castille to Head Fresh Fruit and Vegetable Inspection

Michael A. Castille has been named chief of the Fresh Products Standardization and Inspection (FPS&I) Branch. He succeeds Don Matheson who retired last month.

Mike recently served as head of the inspection section of the FPS&I Branch.

He joined the Federal-State Inspection Service in 1950 as a shipping point inspector and worked in the midwest until 1955 when he became a federal inspector in Chicago. Mike also served as the federal inspection supervisor for Nebraska and Wyoming for three years.

Mike transferred to Washington, D.C., in 1963, as assistant head of the inspection section, and was named head of the inspection section in 1974.

Margaret Hough, secretary-stenographer, was promoted April 27 as secretary to the chief of the Vegetable Branch.

### Grain

Irene Ferrante from clerk to marketing reporter assistant, Market News Branch, Portland, Ore.

Mertin Haggerty to supervisory agricultural commodity grader, Inspection Branch, Indianapolis, Ind.

Rosemary Pollingue to supervisory agricultural commodity grader, Inspection Branch, Houston, Tex.

### Livestock

Donald (Skip) Bevan has been named supervisory meat market reporter in the Washington Market News Branch, replacing Buck Knister, who transferred to the Grain Division. Skip joined the Livestock Division in 1968 and was transferred from the field to Washington in 1972.

### Poultry

Fred A. Pearce, Jr., ACG, Springdale, Ark., was promoted to assistant to the Federal-State supervisor, Arkansas, July 6.

Gerald Y. Robertson, Grading Branch regulatory officer for the Chicago region, was promoted to Federal-State supervisor of Illinois, July 6.

## AWARDS

### Poultry

Frank Santo, Grading Branch regional director, Des Moines, Iowa, was presented with a plaque by the Minnesota poultry and egg industries following his remarks at a seminar June 21. The inscription reads: *Frank J. Santo . . . with deep appreciation for outstanding and dedicated effort . . .. Minnesota Poultry, Butter and Egg Association; Poultry and Hatchery Association of Minnesota; Minnesota Turkey Growers Association.*

## LENGTH OF SERVICE AWARDS

### Poultry

#### 30 years

Lester J. Ames, Grading, Spokane, Wash.

Blanche E. Brashears, Office of the Director, Wash., D.C.

Opie C. Hester, Marketing Programs, Wash., D.C.

Donald R. A. Miller, Grading, Seguin, Tex.

# Personnel Actions

Winfred R. Seaton, Grading, Dalton, Ga.

Henry F. Szetela, Grading, Phila., Pa. (retired)

George W. Taylor, Grading, Mt. Pleasant, Tex.

Devere W. Wenger, Grading, Columbus, Ohio.

Raymond D. Wortmann, Grading, Jackson, Miss. (retired)

## 25 years

George R. Anderson, Grading, Wash., D.C.

Don C. Greenfield, Grading, Dallas, Tex.

Harley Gullord, Grading, Denver, Colo.

Jack W. Mires, Grading, Santa Ana, Calif.

James L. Nicholson, Grading, Marshall, Minn.

Maurice L. Olson, Grading, Marysville, Wash.

Dennis E. Stringer, Market News, Atlanta, Ga.

Donald K. Taylor, Grading, Chicago, Ill.

Carolyn L. Toorean, Grading, Chicago, Ill.

Edward P. Weber, Grading, Bagley, Minn.

## 20 years

Thomas F. Adam, Grading, Cumming, Ga.

Charles Amoroso, Grading, Weimar, Tex.

William A. Bennett, Grading, Salem, N.H.

Donald A. Brinker, Grading, Barron, Wis.

Gordon W. Buck, Grading, Farina, Ill.

Hearld L. Davis, Grading, California, Mo.

Charles F. Goldthwait, Grading, Boston, Mass.

Hartley L. Golly, Grading, Olney, Ill.

Warren D. Golly, Grading, Willmar, Minn.

Howard L. Holm, Grading, Des Moines, Iowa

Joe M. Honish, Grading, Hallettsville, Tex.

Severn A. Jackson, Grading, Hope, Ark.

James E. Kenley, Grading, Zanesville, Ohio.

H. Connor Kennett, Jr., Office of the Director, Wash., D.C.

Earl W. Klein, Grading, Detroit Lakes, Minn. (retired)

Vernon Lowder, Jr., Grading, Little Rock, Ark.

Mary A. Morano, Grading, Phila., Pa.

John B. Osborn, Grading, San Francisco, Calif.

Merrill C. Perdue, Grading, Valders, Wis.

Milton Rosenberg, Grading, Elizabeth, N.J.

Richard A. Shockley, Grading, Harrisburg, Pa.

William D. Talley, Grading, Clarksville, Ark.

Dennis L. Tucker, Grading, Jackson, Miss.

Robert D. Twite, Grading, Willmar, Minn.

James J. Walsh, Grading, Gaylord, Minn.

## 10 years

Alton E. Blakeney, Grading, Collins, Miss.

William E. Creel, Grading, Cullman, Ala.

Lottie M. Crisler, Grading, Pangburn, Ark.

Dallas F. Easley, Grading, Bakersfield, Calif.

Miriam S. Ferrara, Market News, Newark, N.J. (deceased)

Lillian D. Goggin, Grading, Derry, N.H.

Horace O. Holland, Grading, Springdale, Ark.

Billie P. Jimenez, Grading, Los Angeles, Calif.

Ida C. Knopp, Grading, Jackson, Miss.

Henrietta D. Lubetski, Marketing Programs, Wash., D.C.

Janet M. Lupinetti, Grading, Ephrata, Pa.

Ethel W. McCarty, Market News, Atlanta, Ga.

Richard O. Miles, Grading, Yucaipa, Calif.

James T. Nakamoto, Market News, San Francisco, Calif.

John C. Nielsen, Grading, La Habra, Calif.

Bobby C. Porter, Grading, Forest Miss.

Anthony P. Restivo, Grading, Woodbridge, N.J.

Marion E. Spitznagle, Grading, Chesterfield, Mo.

Donald A. Stewart, Grading, Medford, Mass.

Marvin H. Veto, Grading, Middleton, Wis.

Rockley F. Wiese, Grading, Malvert, Iowa.

## Administrative Services

### 25 years

M. Frances Reeve

### 20 years

Thomas Campbell

### 10 years

John A. Bau

Carolyn K. McCabe

Richard E. Walters

AMS Report is published monthly for the employees of the Agricultural Marketing Service of the U.S. Department of Agriculture.
Cheryl A. Palmer, Editor, Rm. 3080-S. Ext. 447-7608
Doris Anderson, Editorial Assistant

# AMS report

AGRICULTURAL
MARKETING
SERVICE

UNITED STATES
DEPARTMENT OF
AGRICULTURE

AN ADMINISTRATIVE LETTER FOR AMS EMPLOYEES

OCTOBER 1975

# Personal from the Associate Administrator

Photo by Lester Shepard

*Associate Administrator John Blum wanted to end his 36-year career with this personal message to his people in AMS, which he considers "the greatest organization in the world."*

Reflection on 36 years of public service produces kaleidoscopic images. Events blend from one to another, each with its own significance. Yet dominant feelings and impressions emerge.

With the exception of three early years in the Bureau of Agricultural Economics and two years of Navy service during World War II, all of my service has been with AMS and predecessor marketing agencies. My feelings reflect this AMS experience.

Surpassing all others is a feeling of personal warmth toward the people of AMS. As I have traveled over the country and visited AMS offices, I have always felt at home, and I have looked forward to the next visit. I shall miss these associations most.

Next is a feeling of pride in the work of AMS and in the professionalism which has been its hallmark. Our programs are important to agriculture and to the public interest. And AMS employees rightfully are recognized and respected for their technical and professional expertise.

Public service is a highest calling. My career has brought me great satisfaction, and if I were doing it over again, there is little I would change. This is a good feeling, and I owe something to each of you in AMS for making it possible.

As to the future, we plan to stay in this area, where family, friends and personal interests are. We look forward to building a 'second home" on property we own on the North Carolina "Outer Banks." And I hope to do some work in areas of professional interest, although plans at this time are not definite.

My heart will remain with AMS, and I shall continue to have an interest in what you are doing. My thanks and best wishes to each of you.                    □

Secretary urged USDA employees to "cross the goal line before that date." ☐

# Division News

## OFFICE OF THE ADMINISTRATOR

### ● Kimbrell Scores in Golf Tourney

With a net score of 66 and a handicap of 18 Assistant to the Administrator **Eddie Kimbrell** walked away with the Administrator's Trophy in this year's ERA (Employees' Recreation Association)-sponsored golf tournament for AMS, FNS, and APHIS. The tournament, which has taken place annually since 1964, was held Aug. 27 at Potomac Park.

## COTTON

● The Division reports with sadness the death of **Melvin D. Stubblefield**, supervisory grader in Blytheville, Ark., who was killed in a plane crash while participating in a Civil Air Patrol exercise on Aug. 23.

## FRUIT AND VEGETABLE

### ● Thomasville Market News Office Goes Year-Round

According to a revised cooperative agreement signed by the state of Georgia and sent to **Administrator Don Wilkinson** for his signature, the seasonal Thomasville, Ga., office started providing year-round market news services on Oct. 1. The seasonal peach office at Macon, Ga., was closed permanently.

The Thomasville office is now responsible for reporting Southeastern (Georgia, Alabama, Mississippi, South Carolina, and Florida) pecans and Alabama potatoes (formerly reported from Birmingham, Ala.); Georgia peaches (formerly reported from Macon, Ga.); Georgia and Alabama watermelons and the National Peanut Report (formerly reported from Washington, D.C., Atlanta, Georgia, and Dalla, Texas). The office now initiates f.o.b. reports on South Georgia vegetables and Mississippi watermelons. **Stanley Cail**, transferring from Birmingham, Ala., is officer-in-charge, assisted by a seasonal reporter during the watermelon season.

### ● Sugar Market News

The Division issued its first *Sugar Market News* report in early September, after taking over the reins for the Sugar Market News program from ASCS on Aug. 1.

**Jim Thorpe**, transferring from ASCS, heads the program, assisted by **Bob Sweitzer**, who transferred from Martinsburg, W. Va., to Washington, D.C. ASCS' **Billy Judge** is on detail to AMS for the transition period, and Billy will be working with Jim and Bob through October.

### ● A Sweet-Talkin' Line

Dial (202) 447-2599 from 3:34 p.m. on any Thursday through 9 a.m. on Friday and you'll get information from the weekly Sugar Market News press release. At any other time the talk is purely honey.

### ● Time for A Change in Florida

A new cooperative agreement signed with the state of Florida has closed the seasonal shipping point offices at Belle Glade, Florida City, Lakeland, and Pompano Beach.

Shipping point reporting duties for all south Florida vegetables are now consolidated at a new shipping point office at North Palm Beach. This office, headed by federal Officer-in-Charge **G.F. Pittman**, also reports the watermelon market for the entire state. The office is staffed with Florida reporter Clad Brockett and three state clerks.

# Division News

According to the agreement citrus activity in Florida is limited to a printed report released by **E.F. Scarborough**, officer-in-charge, Orlando.

The agreement also provides for a new federal-state terminal Market News Office in Miami. **John Engle**, officer-in-charge, Weslaco, Tex., made the initial arrangements for opening the office and turned the reins over to Florida reporter Pam Hill. Pam has completed training on fruit and vegetable reporting at Philadelphia and ornamental crops reporting at San Francisco. The Miami office will report the f.o.b. market for Florida subtropical fruits and ornamental crops, in addition to South American ornamental crops imported through the Port of Miami.

There are no changes in the operations at Sanford and Hastings.

## ● . . . And We Get Coverage

**Bob Criswell**, Minneapolis, Minn., has lined up four radio stations, WVAL, WJON, and WJJO radio in St. Cloud, and KASM in Albany, Minn., to carry the National Shipping Point Trends potato release on weekly farm broadcasts.

The *Center Post Dispatch*, published weekly in Center, Colo., is now showing daily Colorado lettuce shipments and f.o.b. reports on the front page. According to **Clark Price**, officer-in-charge, Denver, the Dispatch also plans to carry the San Luis Valley potato report this fall.

**Les Matherly**, officer-in-charge, Louisville, Ky., reports that WAVE-TV is now including Louisville wholesale market prices for locally grown produce in its daily farm broadcast.

## ● Criswell, Breed to Meetings

**Bob Criswell**, Minneapolis, Minn., attended a meeting of the Minneapolis City Planning Board on July 24. Board members discussed the individual produce dealer's needs for water and electricity on the proposed city produce terminal . . . . Next day Bob attended the Minnesota Beekeepers Association meeting in Brainerd, Minn. Bob made several new contacts for honey market information and became better acquainted with producers currently furnishing him with such information . . . On Aug. 7 **Darrell Breed**, Newburgh, N.Y., spoke to about 80 growers at an Orange County onion marketing conference, sponsored by the Orange County Cooperative Extension Service in Florida, N.Y. Darrell explained market news operations in detail to the growers and they offered suggestions for improving the service.

## ● Colorimeter in Tomato Inspection Activity

Processed products fruit and vegetable inspectors are using colorimeters in California this season for the first time. During a two-year feasibility study, USDA, the University of California, and industry technicians found the colorimeter a reliable aide for visually determining tomato paste color.

*Agricultural Commodity Grader Marie Staub uses Colorimeter to determine orange juice (arrow) color score.*

## ● An Oleaginous Affair

When ASCS contracts to crush approximately 330,000 tons of surplus peanuts into crude peanut oil, as it has this fiscal year, it turns into quite a job for AMS. The Processed Products Standardization and Inspection Branch will inspect the shortening made from the crude oil, as well as the refined oil that will be used in government programs, both domestic and abroad. PPSI people will also determine the condition of the containers, and checkload the domestic shipments.

## ● Gardner Attends Texas Convention

**John Gardner**, chief of the Regulatory Branch, discussed Perishable Agricultural Commodities Act complaint and license matters at the Texas Citrus and Vegetable Growers and Shippers annual convention in Dallas, Sept. 2-5.

## ● Flanagan to Los Angeles

**John Flanagan**, assistant to the chief of the Regulatory Branch, has been temporarily assigned to the Los Angeles Regional Office in California. John is filling in for Tom Walp, the regional director, who is currently absent from his duties for surgery.

# Division News

## GRAIN

### ● Rollin, Leese Escort UPOV Delegation

Stan Rollin, commissioner of the Plant Variety Protection Office (PVPO), met a delegation from UPOV (In ternational Union for Protection of Plants) in Minneapolis in September. The delegates—there were about six representatives from France, Germany, Denmark, the United Kingdom, and Switzerland—were in Minneapolis to inspect research facilities there for developing new plant varieties.

UPOV, according to PVPO Chief Examiner Bernie Leese, is studying the U.S. system for granting plant variety protection rights to see how credible it is. Under the U.S. system for determining whether a plant variety is unique, information obtained through literature searches is programmed into computers.

Under the UPOV system, which is used by all European countries, member countries conduct field tests on the variety in question and study the test results for three years before granting protection rights.

U.S. membership in UPOV depends, in part, on UPOV's accepting the U.S. system.

After the Minneapolis trip, the delgation visited Washington, D.C., and Bernie Leese took them to Niagara Falls. From there they went to Canada, and Stan accompanied them to Geneva, Switzerland, where the UPOV organization is headquartered.

### ● Marshall Is Host to Visitors from Taiwan, the Philippines

John Marshall of the Inspection Branch met with Keith Kelly, assistant director of the Western Wheat Associates, and five flour millers from Taiwan Aug. 22 to discuss inspection procedures for export grain. . . The same subject was the purpose of a visit Sept. 26 of five Philippine contractors of U.S. grain. John said the Taiwan team asked for a sampling demonstration of yellow hard winter wheat, while the Philippine representatives were particularly interested in spring wheat. Both teams wanted to know how to request appeals, and their cost.

### ● Rollin, Leese, Edwards Host Tunisian Seed Team

Under team leader Johnson Douglas of the Ford Foundation, four Tunisian specialists in seed regulatory, seed production, and crop improvement work visited Stan Rollin, Bernie Leese, and Clyde Edwards, chief of the Seed Branch, to discuss their programs. Stan and Bernie explained the work of the Plant Variety Protection Office, and Clyde the federal seed regulatory program.

### ● Crop Survey Team

As a member of a crop survey team, Agricultural Commodity Grader Art Amundson, Portland, traveled to the wheat areas of eastern Oregon Aug. 11-15. The team was under the direction of John Browning, of Western Wheat Associates, who retired from the Division in 1972. The group noted smut problems and other grading factors in the crop.

### ● Senate Subcommittee Public Hearings

J.T. Cosby, Belmer Ekis, and Harlan Ryan, field office supervisors at Cedar Rapids, Des Moines, and New Orleans, represented the Grain Division at Senate Agriculture Subcommittee public hearings in Iowa chaired by Senator Dick Clark. These hearings were held to investigate charges of improper conduct in the sampling and grading of grain by licensed grain inspectors.

## LIVESTOCK

### ● Our Trainees: Where Are They Now?

September was a busy month for the sixteen trainees of the June class. First they met in Washington, Sept. 3-5, for instruction in all aspects of Division activities and AMS' various functions. Then they traveled to the Ohio State University campus at Columbus for extensive training in meat acceptance procedures. Sept. 15 was the day for reporting to official duty stations (their second field locations) where the trainees completed training, as follows:

Daniel Bauder, Sioux City, Iowa; Richard Bloom, Kansas City, Mo.; Ty Brisgill, Bell, Calif.; Eileen Broomell, Denver, Colo.; Nancy Cook, Omaha, Neb.; Gordon Gee, Des Moines, Iowa; Russell Guilfoyle, Omaha; Terry Harris, Indianapolis, Ind.; Douglas Heikel, Dallas Tex.; Danny Mann, Bell; Nora Martin, Denver; Lawson Millett, Amarillo, Tex.; Sharon Neu, Sioux City; Larry Seaton, Sioux City; William Sessions, Cincinnati, Ohio; and Bruce Trainham, Sioux City.

Gordon Gee, Terry Harris, and Bruce Trainham now will be given training primarily in market reporting to prepare for market news duties; all the others will complete their training in meat grading. Two trainees,

# Division News

The Livestock Division's June training class are, from left:

(seated)
Nancy Cook, Eileen Broomell, Douglas Heikel, Ty Brisgill, William Sessions, Gordon Gee, and Sharon Neu;

(standing)
Bruce Trainham, Danny Mann, Nora Martin, Terry Harris, Lawson Millett, Daniel Bauder, Larry Seaton, Russell Guilfoyle, and Richard Bloom.

**Robert Durham** and **Johnny Young**, left the program in August.

The seven trainees in the February 1975 class who completed training in meat grading (one member is assigned to market news) participated in a technical review-of-progress meeting in Denver, Colo., Aug. 12-14, and their formal training is now complete. (Their official duty stations were listed in the special retirements/awards issue.)

### ● Newark & Philadelphia Offices Combine at Princeton; Chicago Market News Office Closes

Use manpower efficiently; offer more effective services; economize! These are mighty tall orders and the principal objectives of several major reorganizations of Division field offices this fall.

The Meat Grading and Market News Consolidated Office at Newark, N.J., and the Market News Office at Philadelphia, Pa., are closing and consolidating into one new office at Princeton, N.J. **George Kablesh**, meat grading main station supervisor at Newark, continues in the same position at Princeton. **Rick Keene** (formerly at Chicago) is market news officer-in-charge at Princeton, assisted by **David Fitzgerald** (formerly at Philadelphia). Both Rick and Dave are responsible for preparing the East Coast Meat Trade Report. The new office location gives market news personnel more flexibility making personal contacts with trade members over the east coast meat trade area from Boston, Mass., to Washington, D.C.

The Chicago, Ill., Market News Office, victim of a declining local meat market, issued its last carlot meat report Sept. 26, and closed its doors Oct. 1. For years after the office issued the first Chicago wholesale meat trade report in 1919, the meat trade there was used as the base for midwest meat prices. The Chicago Information staff wrote the following about the office's close:

. . .the closing of the Chicago office follows the livestock and meat industry's shifting emphasis from Chicago carlot reports as the barometer for Midwest meat prices to meat reports from areas along the Missouri River where production and slaughter occur.

In its broad context, the closing of the Chicago office reflects USDA's continuing recognition of shifts in this Nation's meat marketing system. These shifts are characterized by the meat packers' movement from large consumption centers such as Chicago, to major livestock production areas. This recent shift which is actually a decentralization process, began in the mid-1950's and was highlighted by the closing of the Chicago Union Stockyards in 1971.

### ● Meat Grading National Staff Meets in Sioux City

Meat Grading national supervisors and Branch officials took on a lot when they met in Sioux City, Iowa, July 24-25. They reviewed the technical aspects of grading beef, studied the revised Institutional Meat Purchase Specifications, and discussed management procedures.

Participating were Meat Grading Branch Chief **Dave Hallett;** Assistant Chiefs **Earl Johnson** and **Bob Leverette;** National Supervisors **Ward Stringfellow, Lew Foster,** and **Ed Murray,** Standardization Branch Assistant Chief **Charlie Murphey** and Standardization Specialist **Curtis Green.** Also attending was the Sioux City supervisory meat grading staff, including Main Station Supervisor **Ed Novak,** Assistant Supervisor **Tom Keene,** and Supervisory Meat Graders **Bob Turner** and **Elven Conklin.**

# Division News

The meat grading national staff meets quarterly to maintain accuracy and uniformity in the nationwide application of grade standards and specifications, and to develop more efficient ways of providing grading services to the industry.

### ● Bray Inspects CCC Cattle Exports

**Joe Bray**, reporter-in-charge of the Livestock Market News Office at San Antonio, Tex., examined 22 registered Santa Gertrudis bulls and bred heifers in August at Bay City and San Antonio, Tex. Joe certified these cattle for export to South Africa under the Commodity Credit Corporation's (CCC) Export Credit Sales Program. The Livestock Division—primarily its market reporters—is responsible for assuring that livestock exported under the CCC program meet requirements for breed, age, weight, and body conformation.

### ● Williams, Harding to W. Va. Grading Workshop

**Fred Williams** of the Standardization Branch, and **Bruce Harding**, market news eastern area supervisor, attended the Annual West Virginia Feeder Cattle Grading School, Aug. 11-13, at Charleston, W. Va. Hosted by the West Virginia Department of Agriculture, the grading school helps states coordinate the grading and packaging (grouping by grade and weight) of feeder cattle at state-graded sales.

Fred and Bruce described the USDA grade standards and graded and discussed some 150 feeder cattle. Fred also discussed the Standardization Branch's feeder cattle grade study, being conducted to determine whether current grade standards need revision. About 30 representatives from five states (West Virginia, Virginia, Maryland, North Carolina, and Kentucky) attended the program.

### ● Hallett Addresses Colorado Association; Ferrell Receives Award

**Dave Hallett**, Meat Grading Branch chief, discussed the national meat grading program at the annual Colorado Cattle Feeders Association convention in Vail, Colo., Aug. 15. Dave explained program operations, services, and objectives—to promote an efficient and effective marketing system.

During the convention, **Tom Ferrell**, officer-in-charge of the Greeley, Colo., Market News Office, was given the Association's Top Choice Award for outstanding service to the livestock industry in Colorado. Tom was specifically cited for *outstanding cattle market news reporting.*

*Tom Ferrell (right) receives the Top Choice Award Plaque from Jim Reeman, director of the Colorado Cattle Feeders Association.*

## POULTRY

### ● Kennett and Pepoon in Tar Heel Country

Director **Connor Kennett** and Federal-State Supervisor (N.C.) **Fred Pepoon** attended the North Carolina Poultry Federation's annual banquet in Winston-Salem on Aug. 22. Ticket sales to this affair, which was attended by over 1,100 poultry and allied industry people, are a prime fund-raising method to support the poultry industry in North Carolina.

### ● Egg Research and Promotion Order

On Sept. 29 USDA issued a final decision on the Egg Research and Promotion Order. A referendum will be conducted Nov. 3-28 to determine if eligible producers wish to assess themselves 5¢/30 dozen eggs to operate a nationally coordinated program of research and promotion for eggs, egg products, and spent fowl (nonproductive laying hens). The rate of assessment could be reduced by the Egg Board—the administrative agency that would administer the order—with the Secretary's approval.

### ● Regulatory Officers Update

Poultry Division regulatory officers met for their annual training in Washington, D.C., during the week of Sept. 15. The regulatory officers investigate and follow up on alleged violations of the Egg Products Inspection Act of 1970 and the Agricultural Marketing Act of 1946. Major emphasis at the workshop was put on information needed in preparing cases for possible

# Division News

prosecution—including the accuracy of reports and adequate proof of violations. Attending were **David Olds**, Philadelphia; **Larry Poldrack**, Chicago; **Howard Holm**, Des Moines; **John Osborn**, San Francisco' and **Martin Szekeresh, Jr.**, Sacramento. **Ray Greenfield** and **Joe Beck** (Grading Branch), and **Ora Hopple** and **Merlin Nichols** (Standardization Branch), of the Washington staff, conducted the workshop.

● **Poultry Division on Location**

Division personnel and information specialists have been on location at poultry processing facilities in Virginia to take pictures for two Division slide series. *Poultry Quality Slides* is being updated for training purposes and *How to Buy Poultry* will be added to the Department's list of consumer materials. **Jim Skinner** (Grading Branch), **Merlin Nichols** and **Betsy Crosby** (Standardization Branch), **Sheila Nelson** (Information Division), and **George Robinson** (Office of Communication photographer) visited the plants in August.

● **Egg Slides are Popular**

Sales of Poultry Division visuals were strong during FY 1975. Sales included *How to Buy Eggs* (14 slide sets, 68 filmstrips, and 16 cassettes), and *U.S. Standards for Quality of Eggs* (12 slide sets and 15 filmstrips). Eventually the *How to Buy Poultry* series will also be available as a slide set, filmstrip, and cassette.

● **Hot Line Between Poultry and Livestock**

Livestock Market News Chief **Paul Fuller** and Chicago Livestock Market News Reporter **Rick Keene** visited **Paul Rabin**, officer-in-charge of Poultry Market News in Chicago, on Tuesday, Aug. 19. The livestock folks were interested in the IBM communicating mag card system which has been in operation between the Chicago and Newark Poultry Market News Offices.

● **Egg Products Inspectors Go To School**

**Larry Robinson** and **Bob Anderson**, national supervisors, egg products, Grading Branch, will be conducting a series of schools for egg products inspectors this fall, with the help of the regional supervisory egg products inspectors and federal-state supervisors. The schedule is: Oct. 6-7, Worcester, Mass.; Oct. 9-10, Gloucester City, N.J.; Oct. 20-21, Albert Lea, Minn.; Oct. 22-24, Omaha, Neb.; Nov. 3-4, Chicago, Ill.; Nov. 5-7, Memphis, Tenn.; and Nov. 10-11, Charlotte, N.C. Schools for the western region are tentatively planned for January 1976.

● **Secretaries Are Special**

Eight Division secretaries have attended a Secretarial Institute conducted by Executive Services. The participants, who said the course was very interesting, were **Joyce Carroll**, **Mary Ann Clark**, **Susan Howard**, **Josetta Lamorella**, **Henrietta Lubetski**, **Mildred Mussante**, **Ruth Orenberg**, and **Janet Taliaferro**.

● **"Broiler Marketing Facts"**

*Broiler Marketing Facts—First Quarter 1976*, a quarterly report developed by the Marketing Programs Branch, was issued in September. *Facts* gives the broiler industry an assessment of the major factors affecting broiler marketings to help it plan future production and marketing with expected consumer demand.

According to *Facts*, prospects point to a stronger demand for broilers in the first quarter of 1976 than a year earlier.

● **TV Time Features Chicken**

*How to Buy Chicken*, one segment on USDA's TV program *Across the Fence*, telecast in Washington, D.C., Sep. 13 and 14, was presented by **Betsy Crosby**, Standardization Branch. *Across the Fence* is a weekly 30-minute consumer program filmed and shown in the Washington area, then sent to some 72 stations across the country for airing during the next eight weeks.

● **Skinner on the Circuit for Uniform Poultry Grading**

**Jim Skinner**, national supervisor, Grading Branch, has been real busy with the series of on-site grading exercises he's conducting with the Branch's regional directors, state supervisors, and their assistants. The sessions, held in both turkey and chicken plants, are helping to insure the uniform grading of poultry across the country.

Jim's first trip, in August, was to Indiana. Accompanying him were **Dale Shearer**, regional director (Chicago); **John Cooley**, federal-state supervisor (Indiana), and his assistant **Archie Carver**; and **DeVere Wenger**, federal-state supervisor (Ohio).

Jim's second trip, in mid-September, was to Minnesota. Attending the sessions were **Bill Sutherlin**, assistant regional director (Des Moines); **Don Taylor**, assistant regional director (Chicago); **John Gross**, federal-state supervisor (Minnesota, North Dakota, and South Dakota), and his assistants **Bob Twite** and **Gordy Almberg**.

# Division News

**Herman Schubert**, federal-state supervisor (Wisconsin), and **Ralph Swearngin**, federal-state supervisor (Iowa-Nebraska), also attended.

Jim is planning to head for Arkansas Oct. 20 for the third session in his grading series.

## TRANSPORTATION AND WARE-HOUSE

### ● Audit of Warehouse Service Branch

The Office of Audit has undertaken an audit of the operations of the Warehouse Service Branch. This is a routine check, OA has explained, that's made periodically of Departmental operations. The last audit of the Branch was in 1969. Before the audit began, OA personnel conducted a survey of operations in September to familiarize themselves with the structure, functions and examination procedures of the Branch. The audit will include visits with examiners and warehouses in the field and should be completed about the first of next year.

## INFORMATION

### ● San Antonio Market News 40th Anniversary

Sept. 23 marked 40 years that daily market information has been provided by the San Antonio Livestock Market News Office, operated jointly by the Texas Department of Agriculture and AMS. The event was celebrated by an open house in the Livestock Exchange Building for all patrons who wished to see how market news is collected, summarized, and disseminated.

In special recognition of the anniversary, **Harold Bryson**, regional director of the Information Division's Dallas Office, **Joe Bray**, federal-state market news reporter, and **Loretta Ewart** of the Texas Department of Agriculture developed a news feature for the use of the media. The following paragraphs are highlights from that feature:

*South Texas farmers and ranchers have looked to San Antonio as a major livestock market for more than a century, selling 282,145 head of cattle, hogs and sheep there last year, according to the U.S. Department of Agriculture.*

*Diaries of early settlers, records of livestock sales and other historical documents show that, before the Battle of the Alamo, trading was lively on the banks of the San Antonio river. . .*

*First known pens or livestock years, located just west of the present Bexar County Courthouse, were established prior to 1883. . .*

*Cattlemen organized the Union Stock Yards in 1889 to provide a concentration and selling center where livestock could be properly handled, penned, fed and sold to the best advantage.*

*The yards were located at their present site on South San Marcos street on the two trunk railway lines then entering San Antonio.*

continued next page

*It was horse and buggy days when this picture of the old San Antonio Livestock Exchange Building was taken in the "gay 90's." The many galleries were not only passages, but helped to cool the Exchange in summer. This frame structure was replaced in 1938 by the present air-conditioned Livestock Exchange Building, where the Federal-State Livestock Market News office is located.*

# Division News

The company was reorganized in 1894 with the late Dr. Amos Graves and associates acquiring control. More land was purchased, more pens were built and more facilities were added to what has now become a 38-acre tract.

The Union Stock Yards has remained at this location and in the same hands to the present. It is the oldest stock yards in business southwest of Kansas City, according to Carlton Hagelstein, Jr., president, Union Stock Yards.

Recognizing the importance of the San Antonio livestock market, the U.S. Department of Agriculture (USDA) began reporting daily market news from the yards September 23, 1935 with **Lance Hooks** in charge . . .

disability with 33 years of federal service. Henry was stationed in Raleigh, N.C.

**Joe Mac. Lipscomb** has retired on disability. Joe, an agricultural commodity grader located in Lexington, Ky., joined the federal service in 1968.

## Personnel

**Clarence Brewer**, chief of the Employment and Qualifications Branch retired July 18, after more than 34 years of federal service, all of them with USDA. Clarence began his government service in 1941 with the Office of the Secretary. In 1943, he joined the Bureau of Agricultural Economics, one of AMS' predecessor agencies, in personnel work. He continued to advance in personnel, becoming expert in staffing and placement. Clarence guided the employment branch through the latest reorganization, when APHIS was formed, and can be credited with a smooth and successful transition. Clarence's 34 years of excellent service and his pleasant way of doing business will be remembered and . missed.

# Personnel Actions

## RETIREMENTS

### Grain

**Cecilia Miller**, clerk, Inspection Branch, Duluth, Minn., on disability.

**William Mulloy**, agricultural commodity grader (ACG), Inspection Branch, Seattle, Wash., July 31, after 27 years.

**Ernest Polan**, ACG, Inspection Branch, Chicago, Ill., July 31, after 22 years.

**Betty Waltz**, secretary-steno, Plant Variety Protection Office, Aug. 5, on disability.

### Poultry

**Eloyce Brashears**, administrative management specialist, Administrative Group, Wash., D.C., retired on disability on Aug. 1. Eloyce had served 31 years with the federal government, nearly 18 years with the Division.

### Tobacco

Supervisory Agricultural Commodity Grader **James R. Greene**, of the Lexington, Ky., office, retired with 32 years of service.

**Hilman C. Hicks**, supervisory agricultural commodity grader, has retired from the Raleigh, N.C., office. Hilman joined the federal service in August 1974.

Tobacco Market Reporter **Henry Dickerson** retired on

## WELCOME

### Fruit and Vegetable

**Valerie Emmer**, clerk-stenographer, joined the License Section of the Regulatory Branch, Washington, D.C., on Aug. 25.

**Walter Phillips**, ACG, came on duty in New York City, June 22.

**Thomas E. Robertson**, ACG, came on duty in Newark, N.J., Aug. 31.

**Teresa Sears**, clerk-typist, joined the Fresh Products Standardization and Inspection Branch (FPSI) Miami, Fla., in August. Teresa transferred from the Veterans Administration.

### Grain

**Don Folk**, agricultural commodity aide, Inspection Branch, Des Moines, Iowa.

**Patricia Nugent**, clerk-steno, Seed Branch, Beltsville, Md.

**Lee Sanridge**, ACG, Inspection Branch, New Orleans, La.

**Phillip Tate**, physical science aide, Inspection Branch, Beltsville, Md.

### Poultry

**Danny L. James**, ACG, Arlington, Tex., Aug. 3.

**James N. Overby**, ACG, Platteville, Colo., Aug. 25.

### Tobacco

The following clerks and clerk-typists joined the Division in Raleigh, N.C., over the summer months:

**Nancy A. Bailey**
**Nettie M. Burrell**

# Personnel Actions

Sandra Kay Carnes
Goldie Caulberg
Vera S. Cockrell
Linda C. Medford
Linda C. Parrish
Sandra Partin
John J. Thrower
Betty Wagman
Charlotte Wells
Martha A. Woody

Hortensia B. Mendez joined the Division's San Juan, Puerto Rico office.

## RESIGNED

### Fruit and Vegetable

James Patton, ACG, Newark, N.J. Aug. 29.

Lorraine Silverman, clerk-typist, FPSI Branch, Miami, Fla., Aug. 15.

### Grain

Galen Etie, ACG, Beaumont, Tex.

Cynthia Self, clerk-steno, Administrative Group, Washington, D.C.

Barbara Tipton, clerk-steno, Seed Branch, Hyattsville, Md.

### Poultry

Georgia Grieser, program assistant, Marketing Programs Branch, Wash., D.C., Aug. 15

George Harrell, Jr., ACG, Douglas, Ga., July 19.

Anthony P. Restivo, ACG, Woodbridge, N.J., Aug 8.

## TRANSITION

### Cotton

Harvin R. Smith, Memphis, Tenn., head, Standardization Section to head, Testing Section.

### Fruit and Vegetable

Katie Brubaker, Pompano Beach, Fla., to officer-in-charge, Martinsburg, W. Va.

Stanley Call, Birmingham, Ala., to officer-in-charge, Thomasville, Ga.

Mike Chun, Chicago, Ill., to officer-in-charge, Yuma, Ariz.

Wayne Hobbs, Washington, D.C., to officer-in-charge, Merrill, Ore.

Jack Kerrigan, Merrill, Ore., to officer-in-charge, Grand Forks, N.D.

G. F. Pittman, Washington, D.C., to officer-in-charge, North Palm Beach, Fla.

Bruce Rockey, Yuma, Ariz., to Chicago, Ill.

Bob Sweitzer, Martinsburg, W. Va., to Washington, D.C.

Fred Tennsma, Los Angeles, Calif., to officer-in-charge, Washington, D.C.

Jim Thorpe, ASCS, to Market News Branch, Washington, D.C.

### Grain

Robert Jobb, ACG, Inspection Branch, from Seattle Wash., to Sacramento, Calif.

Mae Parr, personnel assistant, Washington, D.C. Mae was administrative assistant of the regional office, New Orleans, La., when that office closed.

James Vollman, ACG, Inspection Branch, St. Louis, Mo., to Standardization Branch, Beltsville, Md.

### Livestock

Angeline Orzech, writer-editor, Chicago, Ill., Livestock Market News Office, transferred to Poultry Division market news at Chicago, Oct. 1. She joined the Livestock Division in January 1972 after previously working for the AMS Information Division. Angeline has 32 years of government service.

With the close of the Livestock Market News Office in Chicago, Rick Keene, former head of that office, will head the market news side of the consolidated Meat Grading-Market News Office in Princeton, N.J. The former Newark, N.J., and Philadelphia, Pa., offices are being relocated and combined in Princeton.

### Market News Branch

Michael Erwin, meat grader at Fort Dodge, Iowa, transferred to the Market News Branch at Des Moines, Iowa, where he will work as a livestock market reporter.

Jackie Colley - Sioux City, Iowa, to Evansville, Ind.

### Meat Grading Branch

Dean Daniell - Fremont to Minden, Neb.

Emil Slansky - Baltimore, Md., to Bell, Calif.

Wayne C. Zirkelbach - Omaha to Fremont Neb.

### Poultry

The following Agricultural Commodity Graders have transferred:

Loretta M. Adair, from San Francisco to Apple Valley, Calif., Aug. 31.

Donald Alexander, from San Marcos to Lakeside, Calif., Aug. 3.

# Personnel Actions

Betty Lou Barnhart, from Norco to Yucaipa, Calif., July 20.

Daniel S. Capuano, from St. Louis to Sunset Hills, Mo., Aug. 31.

Robert L. Charlton, from Newark, N.J., to Boston, Mass., Aug. 3.

Delmar L. Chipman, from Council Bluffs to Postville, Iowa, Aug. 17.

Ashby W. Franklin, from Arlington to Gonzales, Tex., Aug. 3.

Hillary Gardley, Jr., from Auburn, Ala., to Newborn, Ga., July 20.

Abraham M. Harder, from St. Cloud to Cold Spring, Minn., Aug. 31.

Wayne A. McCarty, from Philadelphia, Pa., to Douglas, Ga., Aug. 13.

Richard Miles, from Yucaipa to La Puente, Calif., July 20.

Raymond J. O'Dell, from Marshfield to Springfield, Mo., Aug. 3.

Richard K. Sands, from Lakeside to San Diego, Calif., Aug. 3.

Arthur J. Storbeck, from Boston, Mass., to Elizabeth, N.J., Aug. 3.

## Information

Carolyn Keene, a secretary with the Information Division in Chicago, has transferred to APHIS.

## DETAILED

### Fruit and Vegetable

Billy Judge of the ASCS Sugar Division is on detail to the Fruit and Vegetable Division for about 90 days. F&V took over the reporting of sugar market news, previously the responsibility of ASCS, on Aug. 1.

## PROMOTIONS

### Fruit and Vegetable

### Market News

H. B. Buchanan, officer-in-charge, Belle Glade, Fla., was promoted and transferred to Philadelphia, Pa.

On Aug. 31 A. Floyd Ermer became officer-in-charge of the Chicago field office of the Processed Products Standardization and Inspection Branch. That position had been vacant since December 1973. Since 1966 Floyd has been assistant officer-in-charge of the Battle Creek, Mich., field office.

Carl Salpietra, officer-in-charge, Philadelphia, Pa., was promoted and transferred to head, Market Reports Section, Washington, D.C.

Leonard Timm, officer-in-charge, Grand Forks, N.D., was promoted and transerrred to assistant officer-in-charge, Chicago, Ill.

### Grain

Les Malone, acting chief, to chief, Inspection Branch, Hyattsville, Md.

Dave Mangum, assistant to the director, to deputy director.

Jon Ruzek, market news reporter, Market News Branch, to assistant field office supervisor, Inspection Branch, New Orleans, La.

Doris Woomer, clerk-steno, Seed Branch, to secy-steno, Plant Variety Protection Office.

### Poultry

Albert B. Kramberg, ACG, promoted and transferred from Elizabeth to Newark, N.J., Aug. 3.

Larry D. Poldrack, ACG, Chicago, Ill., promoted to regulatory officer, July 20.

### Tobacco

Former Assistant Regional Director Paul T. Donovan has been named director of the Lexington, KY., region.

Mary C. Orme, previously a marketing specialist, was named assistant to the director in August.

Louis R. Whiteker has been named supervisory agricultural commodity grader in the Lexington, Ky., region.

## AWARDS

### Livestock

Ed Hulin (left), reporter-in-charge of the South St. Paul, Minn., Livestock stock Market News Office until his retirement in December 1974, was given an Award of Appreciation by the Central Livestock Association in June.

Al Sayer (right) of the Association, who has a daily noontime radio show aired on 15 stations, presented the plaque in recognition of Ed's 15 years (1959-1974) of livestock market

# Personnel Actions

reporting service to the South St. Paul Area. Ed visited 'Big Al'' for 5 to 10 minutes on the air every Friday.

**Margaret M. Hart** and **Sophie M. Healy**, both clerk-typists at the Division's consolidated office at Newark, N.J., were given Certificates of Merit and cash awards in September, *in recognition of special achievement in handling efficiently and accurately an exceptionally large workload, contributing significantly to the effective operation of the Newark meat grading office.*

## Cotton

**Ronald K. Cole**, cotton market reporter, El Paso, Tex., received a quality salary increase and Certificate of Merit for *continuing expertise in the coordination and direction of market news which has significantly increased the effectiveness of the market news services in the western region of the Division.*

## Poultry

**Larry L. Jentsch**, agricultural commodity grader, Wakefield, Neb., received a Special Achievement Award in August for saving the life of an injured employee at the Milton G. Waldbaum Company on March 4, 1975. The citation read: *in recognition of quick thinking and courageous action in aiding a plant employee who was suffocating in his own blood by clearing an air passageway through to his lungs, thereby preventing probable suffocation.*

## Information

**Charlene Olsson**, assistant chief of the Marketing Services Branch, receives a Certificate of Merit from Director **Stan Prochaska** for *continuing exceptional performance in preparing publications, policy statements, and other information materials, and in training new and beginning information specialists.*

Photo by Lester Shepard

## LENGTH OF SERVICE AWARDS

### Cotton

#### 35 years
Glen D. Murrell, Altus, Okla.

#### 30 years
Joseph J. Balkin, Memphis, Tenn.

Luther R. Rone, Alexandria, La.

Gordon H. Schofield, Montgomery Ala.

Lucius L. Wells, Memphis, Tenn.

Roger L. Yoakum, Memphis, Tenn.

#### 25 years
Earl B. Glasgow, Jr., Memphis, Tenn.

Myrthe S. Owens, Augusta, Ga.

Phyllis T. Larsen, Fresno, Calif.

Borden B. Manly, Jr., Abilene, Tex.

#### 20 Years
Jack Cooper, Birmingham, Ala.

Paul W. Karban, Hayti, Mo.

Harold M. Stone, Greenwood, Miss.

Bobby G. Wright, Birmingham, Ala.

Albert D. Peebles, El Centro, Calif.

Glen D. Ratliff, Fresno, Calif.

Ralph G. Rampey, Clemson, S.C.

#### 10 Years
Lorena H. Martin, Atlanta, Ga.

Chester M. Parnell, Greenwood, Miss.

Dorothy T. Picheloupe, Memphis, Tenn.

Donald G. West, Little Rock, Ark.

Archie H. Weatherly, Columbia, S.C.

Margaret V. McMahan, Abilene, Tex.

Joseph N. Rangel, Lubbock, Tex.

Annie R. Brown, Memphis, Tenn.

Doris B. Griffis, Clemson, S.C.

Ethel B. Lampe, College Station, Tex.

It is significant to note that **J. Cooper** and **A. Weatherly** are seasonal employees and earned their 20 and 10-year Length of Service Awards by working only a portion of each year.

**AMS Report** is published monthly for the employees of the Agricultural Marketing Service of the U.S. Department of Agriculture.

Cheryl A. Palmer, Editor, Rm. 3080-S, Ext. 447-7608

Doris Anderson, Editorial Assistant